BOOST
YOUR IQ

"Thinking is the hardest work there is, which is probably the reason so few engage in it."

Henry Ford (1863–1947)

Ron Bracey

BOOST YOUR IQ

Tips and Techniques
for a Sharper Mind

WATKINS
Sharing Wisdom Since 1893

First published 2008 under the title *IQ Power-Up*
This edition first published in the UK and USA 2018 by
Watkins, an imprint of Watkins Media Limited
Unit 11, Shepperton House
89-93 Shepperton Road
London N1 3DF

enquiries@watkinspublishing.com

Design and typography copyright © Watkins Media Limited 2018

Text copyright © Ron Bracey 2008, 2018

Commissioned illustrations: Bonnie Dain for Lilla Rogers Studio

1 3 5 7 9 10 8 6 4 2

Designed and typeset by Clare Thorpe

Printed and bound in the United Kingdom by TJ International Ltd.

A CIP record for this book is available from the British Library

ISBN: 978-1-78678-176-5

www.watkinspublishing.com

CONTENTS

TO TAFFIN, MER MER AND JIMMY,
THE MOST INTELLIGENT PEOPLE I KNOW

INTRODUCTION

From babyhood our intellectual development is monitored to make sure we're making normal progress. During our school years IQ tests may be used to select us for fast-track or remedial teaching and determine whether we enter further education. At work, IQ assessments may be part of the selection and promotion processes. They are also used to diagnose dementia or to measure the effects of brain injury and to monitor recovery; they may even be used to determine whether someone is fit to go to prison.

Even if you're never formally tested as an adult, your intellect, and especially the uses you make of it, has an influence on many areas of your life. It influences the work you do (and how well you do it); it affects your comprehension of what is going on in our fast-moving world and how effectively you are able to interact with its complexities; it even colours, rightly or wrongly, how other people view you and respond to you.

As we shall see in Chapter 1, intelligence can be defined in a variety of different ways, but how has the "intelligence quotient", IQ as a measurement, arisen?

THE EVOLUTION OF IQ

The notion of IQ was developed by Frenchman Alfred Binet in the early 20th century to help determine how much additional educational assistance children with special needs might require. His idea was so successful it quickly came into wider use to assess such things as educational progress and to match people with certain kinds of jobs. A formula for children was devised:

$$100 \times \frac{\text{MENTAL AGE}}{\text{CHRONOLOGICAL AGE}}$$

However, this was not workable for adults, for whom a system of averaging is used (see p.22).

In the course of a century, the concept of IQ has evolved to transcend Binet's narrowly psychometric approach. The idea of the general intelligence factor, or "g", came into circulation at much the same time as Binet's assessment. Although "g" took account of the fact that intelligence is made up of various factors, including heredity, it still missed out the important contributions of social and cultural influences. One development of "g" involved classifying intelligence into fluid and crystallized IQ. Fluid IQ is an innate ability to learn, reason and solve problems, while crystallized IQ is the store of specific knowledge that we acquire through learning and experience.

Two further developments in the interpretation of what constitutes intelligence have had a marked effect in the past 25 years. In his groundbreaking book *Frames of Mind: The Theory of Multiple Intelligences* (1983), Harvard psychologist Howard Gardner introduced the concept that broadened the definition of intelligence from ability with language and logic – the traditional measure of intellectual attainment – to include other manifestations of mental capability, such as spatial, musical and kinaesthetic skills. Then, in 1995, Daniel Goleman's popularization of the concept that emotional maturity is a form of intelligence was so successful that it led to the creation of a new branch of occupational psychology. Emotional intelligence is vital for developing depth of understanding and giving context to intellect, as will be seen in Chapter 6.

NEW FRONTIERS

Just as Gardner, Goleman and others have been re-evaluating the concept of intelligence, technological advances such as magnetic imaging have enabled neuroscientists to see and plot activity in the brain in real time, increasing our knowledge of how we think.

Our understanding of the brain's subtleties and of the relationship between the brain and the mind is still in its infancy, but new discoveries are causing the textbooks to be rewritten. A growing comprehension of the nature of memory has cast new light on the possibilities of improving IQ in adulthood – until quite recently IQ was held to be fixed by the time we leave school. And there is even more recent evidence that the adult brain is capable of what was always believed impossible: regenerating brain cells in a process called neurogenesis.

STRETCHING THE WHOLE MIND

Browse a library or bookstore and you'll find plenty of puzzle books and interactive games to test your logic, numeracy and verbal and spatial abilities. Similarly, a search for "IQ test" on the internet produces thousands of results, providing an irresistible lure if you enjoy testing your mental agility – as you probably do if you're reading this. As the first part of this book explains, such brain stretchers are a good way of honing your skills on tests and sharpening your responses, but they do little to promote an appreciation of the ways in which higher intellectual skills can enrich your life.

Looking beyond the narrow definition of IQ tests, it's possible to apply different intellectual abilities to bring an intelligent approach to all aspects of your life. With the help of the guidance and ideas in this book you can achieve multiple benefits:

- Faster thought-processing skills
- Increased capacity to hold and utilize information in your mind
- An expanded knowledge base, applicable to work, study or leisure
- Improved management of information, so you can filter the wheat from the chaff
- Greater adaptability in adjusting to and accommodating change
- Increased ability to think strategically
- Enhanced problem-solving ability

- Being able to see the bigger picture, the whole issue, rather than just the threads
- The ability to see an issue from multiple perspectives
- Improved confidence in listening to your inner voice and recognizing when to trust intuition.

Few of us make anywhere like full use of our brain's potential resources. This book will guide you through understanding, fine-tuning and enhancing the capabilities of your brain, so that you can make the most of your unique knowledge and insights.

1
EXPLORING IQ

Many of us have faced IQ tests, probably at school and perhaps since, but what exactly does an IQ score indicate, and does it have any meaning and use in adult life?

This chapter looks at the nature of IQ tests, how an IQ value is arrived at, what tests do and don't measure and how to hone the skills required in tests. Finally, there's a questionnaire to reveal your own perception of IQ and a consideration of how refining the definition of IQ can encourage a more rounded view of intelligence.

WHAT IQ IS ... AND WHAT IT ISN'T

Intelligence quotient (IQ) is a measure of the mental skills that psychologists consider to make up intelligence: chiefly, logic, reasoning, quick thinking and knowledge. Testing these skills allows a comparison of intelligence between people. Straightforward? Absolutely not.

DOES IQ EQUAL INTELLIGENCE?

IQ may seem like a fixed entity, because it can be tested and have a value assigned to it. But what has actually been tested, and what does the result show about our overall ability to think and reason?

Even psychologists have yet to agree fully what constitutes IQ and how it can be accurately measured. The boundaries between innate talent and learnt skills are not always easy to define. Ways are constantly being devised to measure subtleties in intellectual ability, and tests are formulated to remove as much cultural bias and ambiguity of interpretation as possible, but difficulties persist in areas such as general knowledge and vocabulary. The relevance of IQ has also been hotly debated because of the implications of reducing so much diversity within a human mind to a single number.

IQ AS A MEASURE OF ACHIEVEMENT

Statistics do provide some generalizations about the relationship between IQ and achievement, and, more negatively, IQ and social problems. High IQ is often expressed in success at school, university and work – people whose IQ scores are in the top 5 percent tend to earn the highest incomes. Conversely, people whose IQs are in the lowest 5 percent are statistically more likely to have social problems, break the law and go to prison: they find life to be more of a struggle.

But, as we shall see in more detail later, an IQ score is based on a fairly narrow range of abilities, while success and fulfilment flow from a wide variety of innate and learnt skills that make us adaptable and effective at what we do. There are people with very high IQs who struggle in life, while more average IQ-scorers achieve success by maximizing their potential. However, this doesn't invalidate IQ tests. While they may not give a complete

10 COMMON MYTHS

You don't have to feel oppressed by the common myths that surround IQ. Here are just some of the things IQ isn't, or doesn't necessarily entail:

- A first-class degree from a top university
- A store of huge amounts of factual information
- Having a phenomenal memory
- Making complex mathematical computations at blistering speed
- Being well-read or able to recite passages of Shakespeare
- Being able to discuss international politics with aplomb
- The guarantee of a high-flying job
- The sole guide to your potential
- A measure of success
- Fixed to your genes or your social or educational development.

picture of intelligence, the skills they measure are important for much more than formal learning and career development.

TESTING IQ

IQ tests come in various guises, from multiple exercises that have been carefully calibrated for medical or educational purposes, to streamlined versions geared to the workplace, to those done for fun. However, they all demand similar skills.

THE WECHSLER SCALE

The most widely used official IQ test is the Wechsler Adult Intelligence Scale (WAIS). This test was devised by American psychologist David Wechsler, who, in 1939, defined intelligence as "the global capacity of the individual to act purposefully, to think rationally, and to deal effectively with his (or her) environment".

This is likely to be the test that is used by medical personnel to assess a patient's intellectual capability – for example, after a stroke or brain injury. A children's version, the Wechsler Intelligence Scale for Children (WISC), is used in schools.

This type of full IQ test is designed not only to assess a person's overall intellectual capacity, but also to show up strengths and weaknesses in specific areas – such as an above-average capacity for logical reasoning or a greater facility with numbers than with words.

To give the most accurate picture possible of mental aptitude, the WAIS tests 14 aspects of ability, divided into four areas, or indexes:

- Processing speed (ability to absorb and interpret information quickly and accurately)
- Perceptual organization (ability to recognize visual patterns and perceive details)
- Verbal comprehension (vocabulary, ability to organize and express information in words)
- Working memory (ability to recall and organize sequences of letters and/or numbers).

Processing speed and perceptual organization are viewed as being largely innate. Verbal comprehension, on the other hand, is highly influenced by educational opportunities, both formal and informal. Working memory, which includes arithmetical calculation and the way we recall things, is something we shall be looking at in detail later, as recent research has shown this to be a key to enhancing IQ potential.

OTHER TESTS

The Wechsler test can only be carried out by specially trained psychologists. The type of tests you're more likely to encounter are those set by MENSA, or the growing number of "recreational" tests available in books or online. These typically cover three aspects of intelligence: language, numeracy, and logic or reasoning. Although they don't carry the weight of a fully controlled test, they are a useful measure of mental acuity.

In addition, it's not unusual for IQ-type tests to be part of a company's recruitment process. These tests are likely to use the same types of questioning and time constraints as IQ tests. They aren't intended to be an exact measure of IQ, but employers and recruitment companies find them a useful tool to gauge, for example, a candidate's numeracy, verbal facility or ability to extrapolate facts from a report.

HOW IQ IS EXPRESSED

To provide a legitimate basis for comparison, IQ tests need to be administered in a strictly systematic way to ensure that everyone has the same experience. The rating for adults is based on an average score for the population as a whole, which is set at 100. The results, plotted on a graph, form a bell curve, with the majority of scores creating the central bulge and the rare cases tapering off at either end (see below). Two-thirds of people fall within the range 85–115.

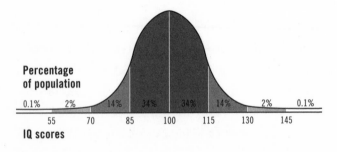

Percentage of population

| 0.1% | 2% | 14% | 34% | 34% | 14% | 2% | 0.1% |

| 55 | 70 | 85 | 100 | 115 | 130 | 145 |

IQ scores

Because the score of 100 is based on the average for a group or population of people, the *actual* intelligence level that it represents can vary. Indeed, it has been observed to change from one generation to the next and from one country to another (see pp.82–3).

Most people don't know their IQ rating: they might simply guess their position on the bell curve according to their attainments in work or school. Many underplay their abilities, or compensate for a sense that their IQ may not be so high by playing to other strengths. This book can help you to improve your IQ score – but, more importantly, it can enable you to use your intelligence as fully as possible.

SAMPLING AN IQ TEST

Whether you wish to perform your best in a job assessment and the like, or just enjoy the challenge of raising your IQ score, it helps to familiarize yourself with the types of questions that appear in an IQ test and understand which thinking skills they require.

THE STRUCTURE OF A TEST

A formal IQ test has several subtests, and is structured to get more and more difficult so that everyone reaches a fail-point at some stage. The questions in "recreational" tests are similar in style, but verbal, numerical and logical questions at different levels are combined within one test. All tests have a time limit, since speed of thought-processing is an aspect of intellectual ability. You might like to try the examples below. Answers not given here are supplied on pp.153–4.

VERBAL

Language-based questions test vocabulary and verbal comprehension. Synonyms and antonyms, word links, "odd one out" questions and questions that test your understanding of the relationships between words are all common. Here are a few typical examples:

1 Underline the word in the following list that is closest in meaning to the word SIMILAR

   close   alike   dissimilar   same   equal

2 Give a word that provides a bridge in meaning between the following:

   free [................] power

3 Thermometer is to temperature as watch is to ....

4 Which of the following is the odd one out?

   drove   swam   travelled   rowed   walked

SHAPES AND SEQUENCES

Language-based tests can be culture-specific, so IQ tests favour figures and diagrams in order to eliminate this bias. Questions like the following employ a series of simple shapes to assess your ability to spot patterns and sequences; to do this, you'll need to understand which rules are being used to create the series, and apply them. Here is one example:

Which shape – A, B, C or D – should come next in this sequence?

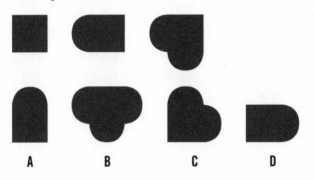

Here the answer lies in seeing that the outlines are formed from basic geometric shapes. The series mutates from a square by the addition of one hemisphere, and then two. So the answer is B, in which a third hemisphere has been added.

The "rules" dictating the pattern could relate to size, shape, rotation, alternation, additions or subtractions, or a combination of them all. The following two questions are more complex examples. Your task here is to identify the rules for each sequence as fast as you can and then apply them.

5   What should replace the question mark?

6   What comes next in this sequence? Is it A, B, C or D?

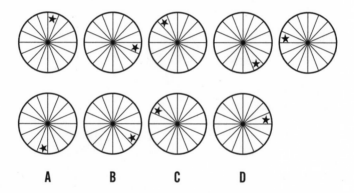

A   B   C   D

NUMBERS

Questions on numeracy are designed to test your understanding of arithmetical functions and basic geometry and algebra, but also to test if you can identify how numbers relate to each other, and find the solution quickly. Some questions require calculation, while others are another form of pattern-spotting. For example:

Which number comes next?

2   4   16   256   ?

Once you've recognized that each number is the square of the number before, you can calculate that the next number will be 65,536 (256^2).

Try the following:

7 Which two numbers come next?

6   5   8   7   11   10   ?   ?

8 Which is the missing number in the sequence?

37   46   ?   129   212

9 What number should replace the question mark in this grid?

B	C	D	D	15
A	D	C	B	17
A	A	A	A	12
B	B	A	A	16

  16 17 15 ?

LOGIC

Some apparently numerical questions are, in fact, tests of logic.

10 Four gardeners can each mow four identical lawns in four hours. How many gardeners (each with their own mower) will be needed to mow 12 lawns in two hours?

Another form of logic question might typically present a series of statements from which you're asked to make a logical deduction.

11 All bricks are made of clay. All clay is hard. Some clay is brown. Which two of the following five statements are true?

A All bricks are hard and brown.
B All bricks are brown.
C Only some bricks are clay.
D All bricks are hard.
E All bricks are clay and hard.

12 A priceless diamond was stolen from a palace by a river. The robber(s) left in a speed-boat. It is known that:

1 No one except Mr Pink, Mr White and Mr Orange was involved

2 Mr Orange never commits a crime without inviting Mr Pink to be his accomplice

3 Mr White doesn't know how to drive a speed-boat.

So, is Mr Pink innocent or guilty?

SPATIAL

This type of question requires you to picture how a flattened shape might be transformed into a three-dimensional object, or, as here, how a 3D shape would appear from a different angle.

13 Which of the following cubes has the same relationship to C as B has to A: D1, D2 or D3?

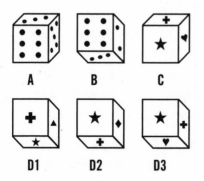

Spatial questions can also involve envisaging how the positions of items can change in relation to each other. Without using pen or paper, how quickly can you answer this?

MENTAL SPEED TRIALS

Many IQ tests demand speed as well as accuracy. In athletics, mere milliseconds separate the world's 20 top fastest athletes in the 100 metres; similarly, tiny differences in speed can have a major effect on mental performance. Practice and the right "mindset" can improve IQ test scores by around 15 points. Try the following activities to sharpen your own mental reactions.

Do IQ-type tests regularly, to help you "tune into" the rules that typically operate in these tests. Computer-based games, and tests in books and magazines, provide plenty of entertaining opportunities to practise.

Polish up your vocabulary and word skills with crosswords, anagrams, "hunt the word" puzzles and games such as Scrabble.

Improve your familiarity with the relationship between numbers – this is often the key to pattern-spotting in sequences. Renew your friendship with times tables, squares, prime numbers. Do kakuro or killer sudoku to help your numeracy and improve your powers of logical deduction.

Practise pattern-spotting. Try making meaningful or silly phrases from the letters in car licence plates or postal codes. Look out for patterns or sequences in telephone numbers or your credit card numbers.

14 You are facing north. You take 30 steps forward, turn east for 30 more steps, turn anticlockwise 45 degrees and pace out another 50 steps. You then turn round and retrace your steps for 20 paces. Next, you turn 90 degrees clockwise and take 40 steps before turning clockwise 45 degrees. Which direction are you now facing?

WHAT DOES IQ MEAN TO YOU?

Before moving on to look at the wider meaning of IQ, beyond the world of tests and scores, try this questionnaire. It will help you to identify the role of IQ in your life, and provide you with a template for personal change.

PERSONAL IQ AUDIT

1: I feel my IQ is ...	
Higher than other people think it is	A
Similar to most people's, but some people are luckier than others	B
Lower than other people think; I just haven't been found out yet	C
To blame for my not having the success that I feel I deserve	D
2: My natural skills show that ...	
I'm good with figures but can never be good with words	A

I'm a good all-rounder	B
I tend to adapt whatever skills I need to achieve something	C
I'm naturally better at communicating than at number-crunching	D

3: At school, I ...

Could have done better but got in with the wrong crowd	A
Enjoyed academic work and focused on getting high grades rather than making friends	B
Felt uncomfortable with academic success, so underplayed my ability	C
Mixed with people who shared my dreams and aspirations	D

4: My attitude to studying is ...

To avoid it because I worry about failing tests	A
I can't see the point of it	B
It's not that important – what you do is more important than what you know	C
That you can always learn new ways of thinking but qualifications don't always mean you can be successful	D

5: My view of reading is that ...

People with a high IQ are well-read	A
Intelligent people tend to read a lot because they are interested in what's going on in the world	B
Normal people are too busy to spend time reading	C
People who are well-read don't necessarily have high IQs	D

6: When it comes to responsibility, I ...

Take on extra jobs at every opportunity	A
Avoid it whenever I can	B
Never seem to get asked	C
Would never take on extra work unless I got paid more	D

7: When it comes to intuition or my inner voice ...

I rarely listen to it when making decisions	A
I feel I just have to do whatever feels OK without over-analyzing the decision	B
I feel my gut instinct is continually conflicting with what logic tells me	C
What's an inner voice?	D

8: My attitude to forward planning is that ...

Living in the here and now is all that matters	A
You have to plan for what you want	B
You have to defer pleasure until you've achieved your goals	C
You need to balance pleasure now with planning for the future	D

9: My outlook on life is to ...

Look forward to the future with optimism	A
See the future as the next five minutes – beyond that is meaningless	B

Believe life is full of luck and fate over which we have little influence	C
Believe we can make our own luck	D

10: With regard to success at work, I think that ...

People in high-flying jobs have the highest IQ	A
It's who you know that determines work success	B
IQ is not as important as the college you attended	C
Successful people often take risks	D

11: On the relationship between IQ and effort ...

People always have to work hard to achieve success	A
Some people are born winners and there's little you can do to change this	B
IQ breaks the link between effort and success	C
You can choose to work more effectively and there are techniques that can help you to achieve this	D

12: Regarding whether IQ shapes who I am, I believe that ...

My personality has no bearing on my IQ	A
I think about everything in life, so IQ plays a role in my relationships	B
IQ is part of me, but it doesn't influence how I relate to other people	C
My IQ determines the person I am	D

13: On the question of how IQ influences my life, I think that ...

It matters at work but not in any other area of my life	A
It's important in determining how I spend my leisure time	B
It's only about thinking – my life is separate from thinking	C
It influences everything in my life	D

14: IQ is ...

Determined by my genes and little can be done to change this	A
Influenced by genes but they don't determine my success	B
A mixture of all sorts of influences, and genetic inheritance is only one of these factors	C
Changed by every experience	D

YOUR SCORES

For each of your answers, find the corresponding score on the chart below. Add up all of your scores. See the next page to find out what your total score shows about your attitude toward your IQ capabilities.

	A	B	C	D		A	B	C	D
1	4	2	3	1	8	2	3	1	4
2	1	3	4	2	9	4	2	1	3
3	1	3	2	4	10	3	1	2	4
4	1	2	3	4	11	2	1	3	4
5	1	4	2	3	12	1	4	2	3
6	4	3	2	1	13	3	1	2	4
7	2	4	3	1	14	1	3	4	2

Personal IQ audit: scores

15–26 You need to build your own understanding of what IQ is and find out how to maximize your skills. You also need to determine your own course in life, rather than attributing your successes and setbacks to external factors. The information on creating a life plan (see p.145) will help you to make your mark on the world around you, and to become less vulnerable to external forces.

27–36 You are more intelligent than you think, but may fail to capitalize on it because you don't have faith in your abilities. When making decisions, apply techniques such as the inference chain (see p.103) to help you explore possible outcomes, and use the questions given on page 72 to help you validate your own intuition.

37–46 You already have the key elements for success in place, so you can gain significant benefits from honing your IQ skills. Relatively small changes in behaviour will make you feel more in control and able to reach outside your comfort zone. You need to build on your knowledge (see pp.92–4) and take responsibility for your decisions. You can do it – just believe in yourself.

47–56 You have excellent insight into the role of IQ in your life, and you use your mental capacity almost to the full. You can further enhance your IQ with the ideas and exercises in this book. Also try learning a new language or playing a musical instrument, which will get both sides of your brain working in harmony (see pp.48–9).

THE IQ CONUNDRUM

IQ tests are a useful measure of certain aptitudes, but they can't tell the whole story about human intelligence. How might our intellectual intelligence be defined beyond the limitations of an IQ score?

INTELLECT AND INTELLIGENCE

There is wide acceptance nowadays of the idea that intelligence might be multi-faceted. For example, the "multiple intelligences" concept identified by psychologist Howard Gardner extends the view of mental capabilities to include kinaesthetic and interpersonal intelligences. However, such aptitudes, while contributing to our nature and abilities as well-rounded individuals, lie largely outside the realm of what are formally defined as higher cognitive skills, such as understanding complex ideas, logical reasoning, planning and problem-solving. These intellectual facets of intelligence are the focus of this book.

CAN IQ BE ENHANCED?

There has been debate for many years about whether pure intelligence – as opposed to learnt ability – can continue to be enhanced once we've reached adulthood.

Science fiction

The possibility of extending human thinking capacity has fascinated people for thousands of years, from the Greek philosophers right through to the pioneers of modern neuroscience.

It's a familiar idea in science fiction, but scientific evidence in the form of a "magic potion" or effective technological aid to thinking is not yet forthcoming. Developments that revolutionize human brain function may lie in the future, but at present neuroscientists offer more cautious suggestions.

Science fact

Potential ways to optimize your IQ can be considered to come in three main forms:

- **Practice** Regular practice is useful for raising your score in IQ tests, and will improve speed and memory capacity. These are important but rather restricted elements of IQ, and don't address skills such as informed judgment and accurate decision-making.
- **Realizing potential** As we shall see in Chapter 2, the balance of the electrical/chemical system within the brain depends on nutrition, exercise, stress control and general psychological well-being. This balance, combined with honing your reasoning skills, overcoming blocks in your thought processes and learning how to think more smartly, forms the basis of optimizing your IQ.

- **Enhancing IQ** It's generally been accepted that a
  child's IQ can be boosted up to about age 13, and to
  some extent up to age 18, but after that IQ is fixed.
  New studies, however, indicate that adults, too, can
  increase their IQ. Specialized diet supplements and
  nootropics (brain-boosting pharmaceutical drugs) are
  being explored, but most exciting is the research into
  the way "working memory" can be used to enhance
  brainpower (see p.96).

The thought that there are ways of actually increasing
your IQ is an enticing one. However, the greatest
difference you can make to your intelligence still lies in
training yourself to use the intellectual assets you already
have to their maximum.

BEYOND THE BELL CURVE

Our performance in IQ tests can fluctuate according to
our level of alertness, our familiarity with the type of
test, or even our mood. This suggests two things: that
an IQ test, however carefully formulated, is a narrow
measure of intelligence; and that if something as simple
as a bad night's sleep can lower our rating, how much
greater our potential might be if we were to realize our
optimum capabilities.

Once you begin to see intelligence as a much broader
concept than your position relative to everyone else
on an IQ bell curve (see p.22), your understanding of

IQ: A MIND-EXPANDING DEFINITION

IQ reflects our capacity to solve problems, think ahead and anticipate the likely outcome of our actions. It also relates to our capacity to filter and integrate a plethora of information, and to deal with the ever-changing world around us. In essence, IQ is the harmonious interaction of a range of thinking and personal skills that makes us effective as human beings.

intelligence will begin to take on a different, and more personal, significance. Maximizing your higher thinking skills can improve your relationships and expand your awareness of your place and purpose in the world, and will greatly increase the possibilities for what you can achieve with your life.

2
THE BUILDING BLOCKS OF IQ

How well our brain works for us is dependent on a host of factors that affect our mental and physical activities, from the connections between our brain cells to the nutrients in our food and the stresses caused by our environment.

This chapter looks at aspects of the brain's structure and functioning that contribute to our thinking processes. The chapter also explores the way in which physical, psychological and environmental factors interact with each other and how all of these factors can be harnessed and enhanced to optimize IQ.

THE INTELLIGENCE NETWORK

Many different elements influence IQ, each contributing something unique toward our intelligence. A weakness in any one area will inevitably make it harder for us to use our intellectual capacities to the full.

VISUALIZING IQ

An immediate way to help you visualize the various interdependent dimensions of IQ is to see it as a net, with each strand as a contributing component. Optimized IQ is achieved when each strand, or factor, is complete, or operating at full strength. But imagine how the net would look if there were weaknesses in one or more strands – the effect would be felt throughout the net, connections would be lost and even strong factors would lose some of their power.

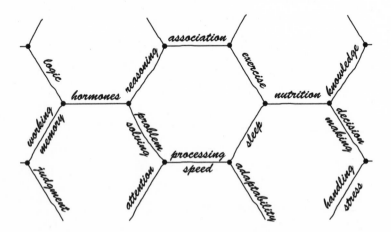

THE MIND–BODY LINK

When the philosopher René Descartes affirmed, "I think, therefore I am," he was succinctly expressing the connection that exists between our mental and physical selves. A range of bodily factors, such as heart rate, blood pressure, muscle tension, sexual arousal and salivation, can be triggered or altered merely by thoughts. But the influence acts in the opposite way, too, with certain pressures on the body affecting the mind.

Imagine how you'd feel after, say, 48 hours without food or sleep: sluggish, dazed and unable to think straight – as if your brain were functioning at half-rate … which, deprived of rest and vital nutrients, is exactly what it would be. This is an extreme example, but deprivation is only a matter of degree: provide your brain with less than optimum conditions and it will work at less than its best, regardless of how intelligent you actually are.

However, before looking at how physiological and psychological factors can be influenced to optimize IQ, we must first take a look at the working of the brain itself.

THE BRAIN AT WORK

Every thought and sensation we experience – whether it's figuring out whodunit or remembering a poem or feeling the heat of a flame – involves the brain receiving, assimilating and passing on information in a lightning-fast chain reaction.

The brain cells that enable this process are called neurons. Each neuron comprises a cell body, a long extension called an axon, and hair-like strands called dendrites. Information in the form of electrical signals passes from the cell down the axon. When a signal reaches the ends of an axon, it triggers the release of a neurotransmitter, a chemical that allows the signal to cross tiny gaps called synapses to the dendrites or body of neighbouring neurons. It is the combination of voltage, speed and synchronization, involving millions of neurons and trillions of synapses, that determines the efficiency of our thinking.

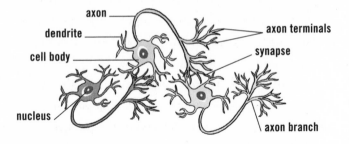

Learning and experience lay down pathways through this neurological system, "hard-wiring" the way we process information. Children's brains do this at a phenomenal rate all the time, but adults are still capable of forging new, smarter connections – it's just more of an effort than following familiar routes laid down years ago. The way in which a brain that has been damaged, for example by a stroke, rebuilds new pathways bypassing the afflicted neurons demonstrates the potential adaptability of the brain to learn new ways of thinking.

Many factors help to keep the system strong and responsive, from mind-stretching games, learning new skills and problem-solving, to physical and psychological well-being.

A BRAIN OF TWO HALVES

The cortex of the brain is divided into two halves, or hemispheres. Each is wired to control the opposite side of the body: the left side of the brain controls the right side of the body, and vice versa. The reason for this arrangement is a neuropsychological mystery, but we know that each side makes very different contributions to the thinking process.

LEFT BRAIN, RIGHT BRAIN

The left hemisphere is language- and skills-focused – this is where we assess information rationally, and where, for instance, those hours of tennis practice get hard-wired into place. The right hemisphere generates more holistic and integrative thought, and is where our creative impetus springs from.

For many tasks, the hemispheres act in concert. They are linked by a thick bundle of nerves called the *corpus callosum*, whose size varies from person to person. Research indicates that the size relates to the strength and speed of communication between the hemispheres.

THE BRAIN IN CROSS-SECTION

LEFT BRAIN

- Knows language
- Is logical
- Is mathematical
- Consolidates past and present
- Puts things in order and sequence

RIGHT BRAIN

- Is imaginative
- Sees the bigger picture
- Sees the present and future
- Is intuitive
- Multi-tasks

Corpus callosum

One study suggests that left-handed people have a larger and more efficient *corpus callosum*, which could give them an advantage in fast or difficult activities that use both sides of the brain. This might explain the significant proportion of left-handers at the top levels of sports and professions such as tennis and architecture.

The co-ordination of left- and right-hemisphere activity demands complex orchestration, achieved by a system known as the central executive. It acts like the chief executive officer in a company: directing thinking, and planning what information is to be processed in which part of the brain, and how. The process happens naturally, but you can improve it by exercising IQ skills.

INTEGRATED THINKING

Creating a harmonious interplay of left- and right-brain functions is essential for enhancing IQ. Drawing on the strengths of both sides to work out a problem, or to evaluate or retain information, can deepen understanding, speed up thought processing and improve memory.

You may have noticed how information becomes easier to digest if you see it as well as hear it – for example, when a news report is backed up by photographs or maps. This multi-modal representation engages both sides of the brain: the left hemisphere triggered by the words you are hearing and the right by the pictures.

PRACTISING INTEGRATED THINKING

The following exercises will encourage you to work both sides of your brain together.

- In this exercise, called the Stroop Test, you use coloured pencils to write the names of colours, each in a colour different from the one named by the word: for example, GREEN in red pencil. Read the words, then try saying the colours that you see, not the words. (You can also find many examples of this test on the internet.)

- Imagine objects, or even organizations, as animals. For example, "my cup looks like the sucker on an octopus's tentacle," or "that company is like an angry rhinoceros smashing into the trees."

- Try writing or drawing with your "wrong" hand (your left hand if you're right-handed, and vice versa). Notice how this feels to you, both physically and mentally.

WORKING MEMORY

The capacity of our working memory is strongly linked to overall intelligence, and in recent years it has been shown that this capacity – and therefore intellectual ability – can be increased in adults as well as children.

WHAT IS WORKING MEMORY?

Working memory has been described as another label for short-term memory. However, as we often use "short-term memory" to mean memories of the recent past ("what I had for dinner last night", "why I came upstairs"), which are actually memories lodged recently in our long-term memory, this is not a useful definition.

Working memory is actually what enables us to hold on to and manipulate information in our minds. We use it, for example, to press the right buttons for a phone number we've just been given, to do mental arithmetic calculations in our heads and to make sense of the flow of a conversation or debate. Working memory might be considered a "holding bay" for information which can then be acted on, discarded or stored in long-term memory.

HOW DOES WORKING MEMORY WORK?

Working memory is directed by the brain's "central executive" (see p.48), which sends the sensory, verbal or other information it receives to be processed in one of two systems within the brain. Words and numbers that we read or hear, for example, are processed in the left hemisphere's "phonological loop", while visual or spatial information, such as where you are on a page or the shape of something, is processed via what is called the "visuo-spatial sketch pad" of the right brain.

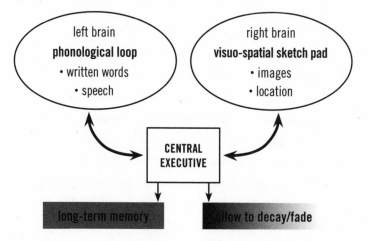

These two systems don't work in isolation, however, and the central executive co-ordinates the input of both to process information. So, for example, reading a map calls for taking in and manipulating verbal information (street names) in co-ordination with visual information (the relationship of one street to another).

WORKING MEMORY IN ACTION

Our working memory can generally hold information amounting to seven "pieces" of data, such as the digits of a telephone number. You can test this fact for yourself: ask someone to recite a string of random numbers to you, and see how many of those numbers you can repeat back to them. Then do the same exercise again, but try reciting them back in *reverse* order. Most people can manage to remember about seven numbers going forwards and five numbers backwards.

Think about how you were able to do this. You probably found yourself saying the numbers to yourself – this is the "rehearsal" element of the phonological loop. However, when it comes to recalling a number sequence backwards, particularly if you ventured beyond four or five digits, you probably visualized the numbers, as if you were seeing them written down. By doing so, you're pulling your visuo-spatial sketch pad into the process.

Because your working memory is a processing faculty, not just a "storage facility", improving it can have a positive impact on broader intellectual ability. In Chapter

4 you can find practical ideas for building up your working memory (see pp.96–8).

FEEDING THE MIND

Research has proved the correlation between food and IQ in children: it was found that youngsters who had impoverished diets made major gains in mental function once they started to have balanced meals.

An increasing amount of evidence is emerging that better nutrition can improve thinking skills at any age.

FUNCTION FOLLOWS FOOD

Two of the main physiological systems that determine the overall functioning of the brain are:

Metabolism All the chemical processes that occur in the body, including those that convert food into "fuel" for the body and brain

Nervous system The brain, nerves and neurone pathways, with which we make associations, form memories and process information.

Thinking processes are mediated by four key neurotransmitters, or "chemical messengers", that act on the neural pathways (see pp.46–7); they are listed below. Certain foods are particularly rich sources of these chemicals.

- **Dopamine** regulates attention and motivation, and prompts the brain to focus on seeking material or psychological rewards.
  Good sources: dark chocolate, chicken, oats.
- **Acetylcholine** regulates the processing of sensory information and helps the brain to encode and access memories.
  Good sources: eggs, avocados.
- **GABA** controls the levels of other neurotransmitters in the brain and helps to regulate anxiety.
  Good sources: almonds, broccoli, walnuts.
- **Serotonin** regulates mood and helps to limit impulsive behaviour.
  Good sources: turkey, bananas.

GLUCOSE: THE BRAIN'S FUEL

Glucose is derived from carbohydrates and the brain doesn't differentiate between sources – wholegrain rice, a spoonful of honey or a bar of chocolate are all equally valid supplies. The only difference is in the speed with which it reaches the brain, so forms of simple carbohydrates, such as fruit and sweets, and sugar itself, are very quickly absorbed, while extracting and processing glucose from complex carbohydrates, such as pasta, cereals and potatoes, is a slower process. The first provides the brain with a sudden boost (the "sugar rush") while the second is more like a drip feed.

Whereas our bodies can draw energy from stored fat, the brain is unable to store glucose, so it needs a constant supply. However, too much all at the same time can be as detrimental as glucose starvation – the hyperglycemic and hypoglycemic comas of a diabetic are dramatic examples of the effects of such a feast or famine.

Something as simple as missing breakfast can interfere with glucose metabolism and reduce brain electrical activity, so start the day with a breakfast that will slowly and steadily supply glucose to your body and brain. This means a meal that is high in complex carbohydrates such as wholegrain cereals and bread. Studies have shown that a diet high in refined carbohydrates such as white flour and sugar can reduce IQ functioning by as much as 25 percent by interfering with the insulin/glucose balance.

Maintaining a regularized "drip feed" supply of food for the brain will also help you to avoid the common experience of a mid-afternoon dip, when your physical and mental energy flags.

A BREATH OF FRESH AIR

Another vital substance for the brain is oxygen – and one of the best ways to increase your oxygen intake is by exercising. Physical activity improves all body functions, including blood flow (which supplies the brain with oxygen), glucose metabolism and neurotransmitter activity. Regular exercise has a positive effect on mood, concentration and alertness. It also promotes a healthy sleep pattern, which in turn gives rise to a more alert mind and faster thought-processing.

Introducing more physical activity into your life doesn't have to mean regular sessions at the gym. You're most likely to stick at something if you enjoy it and it suits your lifestyle, whether it's a brisk walk every day or a kick-boxing class.

THE POWER OF LAUGHTER
A good laugh can supply physical as well as psychological benefits. It makes you breathe more deeply and take in more oxygen. It also relaxes your muscles, lowers blood pressure, reduces stress and gives you a sense of well-being. Laughter can have a beneficial effect on mental skills: a joke, or a funny view of a subject, can free up your thinking and point the way to a wider view or new understanding of the issue.

BRAIN-BOOSTING SUPPLEMENTS

Every week there are claims and counter-claims for specific foods and supplements that enhance (or harm) the working of the brain. Nutrients work in complex ways and in concert with each other, so it would be simplistic and wrong to say that just an extra dose of X or Y will enhance brainpower. However, certain nutritional components known to have a particular effect on the brain's function include:

- **Omega-3 fatty acids** These belong to a group of nutrients called essential fatty acids, which help to maintain cell membranes and improve blood flow. Studies show that omega-3 fatty acids may improve brainpower. Foods rich in omega-3 include linseed, walnut and rapeseed oils and oily fish (which perhaps lends truth to the saying that fish is good for the brain).

- **Vitamin B_{12}** This vitamin helps to maintain healthy nerve cells. Deficiency has been associated with impaired memory or even a form of dementia (reversible if treated early enough). Vitamin B_{12} is found in a wide range of fish, shellfish and meat (especially liver), and to a lesser extent in dairy foods, but not in vegetable matter except for seaweed – vegans (who eat no animal products) need to take it as a supplement.

- **Caffeine** Found in coffee, tea, cola and chocolate, caffeine is a mental stimulant. Just two cups of coffee can boost working memory in the short term, and may improve mood and attention. Caffeine also triggers the release of dopamine (see p.54), mostly in the frontal areas of the brain. However, excess caffeine can raise anxiety levels, disrupt sleep and aggravate depression.

PSYCHOLOGICAL INFLUENCES

The link between how well our brain functions and our state of mind is not always obvious, but understanding the influence of factors such as mood and personality can help you to enhance the flow of your thinking.

FIXED AND TRANSIENT FACTORS

Our ability to think clearly is influenced by a host of factors in our internal and external environment. Internal factors include our mood and attitudes; external factors include the amount of information available to us or the quality of our social interactions.

The table below shows some of the factors that can affect our thinking ability. Some of these factors are relatively stable and stay much the same throughout our lives, but others are more fluid: they may be either changeable in nature, or come and go according to circumstances. These are also sometimes called "situational" factors. Yet other factors fall between the two types. It can help to be able to identify when particular factors are affecting you, so you can take appropriate action: for example, by doing something enjoyable to relieve stress or lift a low mood.

STABLE	MIXED	FLUID/SITUATIONAL
Personality determines your level of motivation, reaction to failure, and desire for success	**Attitude** determines your perception of the likely benefits and risks of particular activities	**Mood** affects your confidence and expectation of success while you're engaged in a task
Handedness has an influence on your predominant mode of thinking (see p.48)	**Intuition** depends on your ability to listen to your inner voice and judge when to act on it	**Stress** from external factors such as noise or poor relationships can hamper your activities

IQ AND FLOW

Flow is an important concept in the emerging science of positive psychology. It describes a state of optimal psychological effectiveness, in which you're working at the peak of your abilities. It can occur when you're engrossed in an activity that you're good at, and your thinking seems clearer and more inspired than usual. You become so engaged in the process that you feel full of energy, you lose track of time, and you have a sense of utter peace and control over the task.

Flow is something you can recognize as having after the event, like concentration, but once you recognize you have it, it's gone. Such an enhanced state of thinking is not always easy to attain, although certain conditions facilitate maximum flow (see opposite).

Many workplaces, which would benefit from encouraging employees to greater intellectual heights, often seem to provide environments that militate against any possibility of flow, which is ironic as this is detrimental to both productivity and creativity. Interestingly, employees are beginning to recognize the advantages of working for organizations that are more flow-centred.

CREATING MAXIMUM FLOW

The circumstances conducive to optimum flow are not the same for everyone. As you experiment with settings and conditions, take the following into consideration until you find the combination that most encourages you to enter a state of flow.

Setting
Make sure that lighting, seating, heating and general ambience are all tailored to your preferences.

Distractions
Stop all interruptions and any unwelcome noise. This doesn't necessarily mean silence: you may find that particular background noise or music (see pp.80–1) helps your flow.

Psychology
Set yourself a realistic but challenging deadline – often, a mild external stressor like this can help to concentrate your mind. Focus on your strengths, so you have a high expectation of success, and suspend any fears or negative thoughts about the outcome.

Physical
To achieve a flow state, you need to have rested and supplied your brain with the glucose it requires, so make sure that you've slept and eaten well. Some people will think faster with a caffeine lift.

3
THINKING ABOUT THINKING

How we think can help or hinder us in using our intelligence. IQ performance has a lot to do with our state of mind, as well as our mental skills.

This chapter starts with an essential element of learning and intelligence: "metacognition", or awareness of our own thought processes. It goes on to look at the way in which our subconscious can influence how we perceive problems and intellectual challenges, and how we can set up mental barriers that prevent us from reaching our full potential. It also explores logic, seeing the broader view of an issue, and ways to focus attention – abilities that will take you beyond the specific skills needed to pass IQ tests, to boost your general intelligence and enhance every area of your life.

METACOGNITION

One of humanity's defining characteristics is our awareness of the thinking process itself – the knowledge of how we might tackle a problem or, retrospectively, how we've reached our solution. The psychologists' term for this awareness is metacognition.

THINKING ABOUT LEARNING

Metacognition is "thinking about thinking". Whereas cognition, or straightforward thinking, is what happens as you apply your mind to a new issue, metacognition is the act of assessing *what* you're thinking and doing in the course of this process. It is particularly associated with learning and problem-solving.

We all use this technique every day – not just at work or when studying, but in common tasks such as trying out a new recipe or driving through an unfamiliar area. If we start thinking about how we think, we can think more effectively and take a more objective view.

APPLYING METACOGNITION

Metacognition involves knowledge of yourself (including factors that might distort thinking) and control of the process. The latter includes how to plan, carry out and evaluate your course of action. First, define the nature of the challenge (see p.105), then follow the process in the chart opposite. Work through the questions for each stage to gain more control over your tasks.

Planning	What existing knowledge and skills can I apply to this task?
	How much time do I need for it?
	What materials or resources do I need?
	Which tasks need to be done, and when?
	What should I do first?
Monitoring	Am I on the right track, or do I need to alter my approach?
	Do I need to go faster or slower?
	Has the situation itself changed since I started?
	What do I need to do if I encounter any difficulties?
Evaluating	How did I do? – as well as I expected, better, or worse?
	Which of the things I did were successful/helpful?
	What could I have done differently?
	How can I apply what I've learnt to future situations?

Intelligence tests are a great way to exercise meta-cognitive skills. Relax, and treat the tests as a game. It helps to know what type of skill is needed in each question: logic, pattern recognition, and so on. You then get into the frame of mind that you'd assume in a game involving that skill – for example, you might approach a logic question in the same spirit as you'd approach a sudoku puzzle.

When learning or reading new material, possible metacognitive techniques include asking yourself questions as you go along: "Do I understand this?"; "How would I describe this to a friend in a conversation?" It's also helpful to understand your characteristics as a learner – ask yourself how you digest information most effectively – and then plan your study around those characteristics.

SUBCONSCIOUS INFLUENCES

Much of our thinking goes on below our conscious awareness. If you can understand how your subconscious mind influences your views, you can harness its power and at the same time avoid the traps into which it can lead you.

YOUR INNER VOICE

The subconscious stores our most basic instincts and is the seat of deeply ingrained patterns of thinking (see pp. 138–41). Lessons learnt long ago and lodged in the subconscious give rise to our inner voice: intuition. This voice can be a great help – allowing you to find information instantly because you "just know" what's right – but it can also be misleading.

We're constantly updating and revising our view of the world, drawing on previous experience and logical reasoning. But sometimes our logic can become skewed if it's based on a faulty interpretation lodged in our subconscious. Examples of such distortions include:

• A habitual response based on an outdated assumption: "I won't be able to understand what my bank manager is talking about because I was never any good at mathematics at school."

• Overgeneralization: "I can't believe what she says, because politicians never tell the truth."

The next pages look in more detail at factors that can impair your thinking, and at how to sharpen your perceptions and objectivity.

LEARNING TO THINK STRAIGHT

Past experience affects how we handle new information or resolve new questions. By recognizing habitual distortions in our thinking, and taking steps to correct them, we can increase our chances of a fresh, accurate approach, including unlearning our habitual assumption that some intellectual challenges are beyond our reach.

DEALING WITH DISTORTIONS

Habitual distortions in the way we think about ourselves can undermine our brain power unnecessarily. If we have a low opinion of our own intellectual capacities, this may act as a self-fulfilling prophecy, undermining our confidence and in turn leading to a poor performance in a particular mental challenge. Through experience we form mental frameworks called "schemas" to guide us automatically through a wide range of regular events – everything from doing the household accounts to engaging in a political discussion with friends over dinner. But not all schemas are helpful: they can distort our perceptions in ways that lead to underachievement.

IDENTIFYING NEGATIVE SCHEMAS

American psychologist Jeffrey Young defined 18 possible negative schemas, grouped into five key areas, which relate to our relationships with ourselves and other people (a common cause of stress).

Some of these schemas have a bearing on the use of the mind. By considering their influence on your thinking, you can identify any factors that could be preventing you from optimizing your intelligence.

The pairs of statements A–E that are shown in the chart on the opposite page represent the five key areas in Young's schemas. Read each statement and then give it a score, according to the scale, and note it in the blank left-hand column.

Add each pair of scores and then write down the total in the blank right-hand column after the statement. A high score in any key area indicates negative thought that you need to release.

Key area A: Rejection and detachment
A high score in this area suggests that you feel inferior to other people, so lack the confidence to explore your own capabilities.

Key area B: Impaired autonomy
If you scored highly here, you hold a deep-seated belief that you're a failure. This can torpedo any plan or action before you even start.

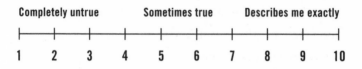

		Completely untrue	Sometimes true	Describes me exactly
		1 2 3 4 5 6 7 8 9 10		

A	I'm not as clever as other people.	
	People would think less of me if they knew how stupid I am.	
B	Almost nothing I do at work (or school) is as good as what other people can do.	
	It's no use trying to achieve things, because I'll fail.	
C	I can't force myself to do things I don't enjoy, even when I know it's for my own good.	
	If I can't reach a goal, I get easily frustrated and give up.	
D	I feel I have no choice but to accept other people's ideas, even when I'd like to express my own.	
	I have to do well for the sake of my colleagues (or family).	
E	I must always do my best; I can't accept mistakes.	
	I feel there is constant pressure for me to get things done and fulfil my responsibilities.	

Key area C: Impaired limits

If you noted a high score in this area, you might lack discipline and self-control, thus stopping yourself from attaining long-term goals.

Key area D: Other-directedness

A high score for these questions indicates that you rely too much on other people's approval, at the expense of your own self-development.

Key area E: Over-vigilance and inhibition

If you scored highly on this pair of questions, you hold yourself to punishingly high standards, and don't allow yourself the freedom to experiment, make mistakes and learn new things.

Try to assess how your negative schemas might be influencing the ways in which you think and learn: do they really reflect what's going on in your life now? Identifying unhelpful patterns of thought and putting them into context should help you to spot when faulty or outdated assumptions are distorting your thinking.

BOOSTING CONFIDENCE

Often, we hold back from using our full intelligence because we fear what others might think, or dread making mistakes. Underlying these anxieties is pressure to meet the standards of our worst critic – ourselves.

THE ANXIOUS INNER VOICE

It's not surprising that we care what other people think of us – most of our moral awareness develops from appreciating the rules of social behaviour. However,

EDUCATED OUT OF THINKING?

Schools, colleges and workplaces teach us certain essential qualities, such as discipline and perseverance. However, all too often they can also crush our confidence and stifle our natural intelligence. If you've suffered this experience, you don't have to let it limit you for life: see below for possible problems and ways to overcome them.

Conformism The idea that there are absolute right and wrong ways to do things can discourage you from "thinking outside the box", so that you focus on obeying the rules and restrict your own vision for the future. Refer to pages 74–6 to help you see the bigger picture of your life.

Rigidity of outlook The promotion of narrowly academic skills comes at the expense of building other aptitudes, such as emotional intelligence. See pages 138–41 to help you understand how reasoning skills work together with emotion and intuition to form our unique intelligence.

Pressure to achieve An emphasis on exams can lead to anxiety and defensive thinking, instead of curiosity and the will to stretch yourself. Pages 59–61 show you how to get into the "flow" state, where you can overcome anxiety and enjoy working at your optimal capacity.

Negative categorization Grading can have the effect of sorting people into "successes" and "failures"; and being made to feel like a failure can inhibit you from using your talents fully. See pages 68–70 on how to identify and overcome negative self-appraisal. See Chapter 4 for how to build knowledge and enhance your confidence.

sometimes concern about the view others have of us becomes serious enough to restrict our daily lives. For example, it may be the zipper that keeps our mouth shut during meetings, preventing us from voicing ideas in case other people ridicule them.

TAKING A MORE OBJECTIVE VIEW
By separating out the facts of a situation from your own and other people's opinions, you can view it more objectively – and perhaps more fairly to yourself.

Think of a situation in which you achieved something that made you feel proud, and a situation in which you failed to achieve a hoped-for goal. Then answer the following questions:
- How did you know whether you'd succeeded or failed?
- How did you feel in each situation?
- How did people around you react to what you'd done?
- Which of these three factors had the strongest effect on your feelings of success or failure?

LOGICAL REASONING
Logic – the system of reasoning that enables people to construct sound arguments – was a subject for formal study in classical education. It is a major element of IQ, and is key to our ability to reach accurate conclusions from facts.

FORMS OF REASONING

What we normally understand as logical reasoning is a line of thought that proceeds from accurate premises (initial observations), via rational inference (the meaning we draw from our observations), to a true conclusion. There are two main forms: deductive and inductive.

In deductive reasoning, the conclusion follows inevitably from the premises. If the premises are true, the conclusion must also be true. One famous example goes as follows: "All men are mortal; Socrates is a man; therefore, Socrates is mortal." However, it's perfectly possible to reach a valid conclusion from false premises, as in, "All men are amoebas; Socrates is a man; therefore, Socrates is an amoeba."

In inductive reasoning, if the premises are true, then the conclusion is highly likely to be true. For example: "The sun has risen every day for the past 4.6 billion years, so it will rise again tomorrow."

HOW ERRORS CAN ARISE

We like to think we're basically rational beings, but it's easy for us to misinterpret what we observe, or to draw wrong inferences from facts. Organizational psychologist Chris Argyris coined the expression "ladder of inference" to describe the steps that can lead from established fact via shaky supposition to fiction (see box, overleaf). We can run up the rungs of the ladder in a flash without realizing it.

THE LADDER OF INFERENCE

From an established or observable fact (on the bottom rung), we typically select a detail onto which we impose a subjective meaning or inference. That then becomes the basis for an assumption, which gels into a firm belief on which we base further beliefs or actions. For example:

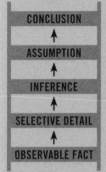

Conclusion: The Earth is at the centre of the universe.
Assumption: The Sun circles around the Earth.
Inference: The Sun is moving.
Selective detail: The Sun appears to be moving.
Observable fact: The Sun rises in the east and sets in the west.

It's easy to spot the false step, but for thousands of years humankind accepted the faulty inference, and from it built up a wholly mistaken construction for the universe.

Knowing the principles of reasoning will help you to distinguish good arguments from poor ones. On pages 99–100 you'll find exercises to help you identify faulty thinking. The inference chain on page 103 will enable you to check each stage of your reasoning processes.

THE BIGGER PICTURE

An essential aspect of intelligence is the ability to respond to a complex, changing environment: looking beyond present concerns to see the bigger picture, and making connections with situations you've already encountered, or things that you've learnt. "Bigger picture" thinking stretches your mind.

RECOGNIZING PATTERNS AND THEMES

Imagine that you're standing right next to something very big hidden under a sheet, and you're asked to identify it. The sheet is removed, but all you can see is an expanse of leathery greyness. The sheet is replaced; you move around to another part of the object, and the shape is uncovered again. This time you see a hard, curved thing. You're none the wiser. The sheet is replaced, and removed again. This time you step back. Now, with a more complete view you can see that the mystery object has a trunk and tusks and two big ears.

Sometimes we're overwhelmed with detail and we "can't see the wood for the trees". Being preoccupied by minutiae can cause us to overlook or misinterpret vital information.

Imagine how you'd describe an elephant to someone who'd never seen one. What would you mention? The huge size? The trunk? The big ears? The fact that elephants live in herds?

Where elephants live? All of these elements are interrelated, and help to build up a full picture of an elephant. This type of thinking, called systems thinking or holistic thinking, can enable you to expand your network of knowledge.

ENLARGING THE PICTURE FRAME

When tackling a specific challenge or course of action, apply holistic thinking to broaden your view. Consider how the issue fits into your life as a whole, and how you can create an "environment" for success.

- Incorporate the issue into your normal activities. For example, if you're learning Italian, write shopping lists in the language.
- Look at your issue from the viewpoint of someone completely unlike you: a child, say, or a hill-farmer. What ideas might they come up with to help you?
- Try drawing a picture to illustrate what you're attempting to do. Or try acting it out as a charade.

DEVELOPING VISION

To apply your intelligence in this ever-changing world, you need to have vision: the ability to anticipate consequences, adapt to changes and plan for the future. It's like playing a game of chess in four dimensions – one of which is time.

THE LONG VIEW

Most definitions of intelligence include the capacity to plan ahead and to visualize consequences – or possible alternative consequences. This applies just as much to "real life" as it does to abstract cerebral activities such as planning the next moves in chess. For example, a company's chief executive officer needs is vision to make decisions that will play out over months or years, and predict the likely impact of these decisions.

OPENING OUT YOUR PERCEPTION

In intelligence terms, a capacity for forward planning is tied closely to the ability to learn from past experience. It's natural for us to see life as a simple, linear route on which we face the future and have our back to the past. However, what we've learnt in the past and what we're planning for the future are inextricably linked to the present. So it would be more accurate to imagine the straight line of a life's path opening out like a fan, with the present as the hinge point of the fan, and the past and future as the interlinked and interdependent ribs.

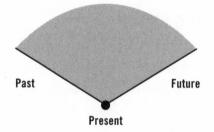

Past   Future

Present

Another way to envisage this is to imagine hovering in a helicopter and seeing your life spread out below you. This "helicopter view" puts things in perspective, allowing you to appreciate how the past and present fit into the bigger picture of the future.

SEEING THE WAY AHEAD

The unforeseen will always occur, but it is possible to train your mind to see the way ahead more clearly by:

- Developing an ability to marshall facts and distinguish the important from the unimportant
- Holding in your mind the bigger picture (see p.74) while not ignoring details that can make a difference
- Recognizing how what you already know can apply to new circumstances or problems
- Learning when logical deduction points the way forward and when intuition should be noted (see Six Hats thinking, p.118)
- Visualizing the knock-on effects of different outcomes.

You can actually apply the skills required in IQ tests to test your ability in many of these aptitudes.

FOCUSING YOUR ATTENTION

The ability to change your level of attention – to expand or deepen your awareness – enables you to perform a wide variety of mental tasks. There are various ways in which you can consciously alter your level of attention. These methods, if used regularly, can greatly improve your cognitive skills.

TRAINING THE BRAIN

The brain has different levels of electrical activity, which suit different types of task; these levels can be shown on an electroencephalograph (EEG) reading, as waves:

Beta waves are associated with concentration and logical thought

Alpha waves indicate relaxed alertness and holistic thinking

Theta waves relate to meditation, visualization and creativity

Delta waves are primarily associated with deep sleep.

In a technique called neurofeedback, people are taught how to influence the EEG readings (which entails altering their brain waves) by conscious thought. However, there also exist much older methods of consciously altering your brain function.

In mindfulness (see box overleaf), you quietly turn your focus away from your thoughts, and expand your attention to take in everything that's going on around

BE HERE NOW
The concept of mindfulness, or "being in the moment", originated in Buddhism, but can be utilized by anyone. By practising it regularly, you can sharpen your awareness and clear your mind of clutter, thus increasing the power of your thinking. Try the following simple exercises:
- Sit quietly, and for one minute focus only on your breath. Whenever a thought or feeling arises, simply accept it as it is, and then let it go.
- If your mind goes blank in a meeting, quiet your thoughts and then tune into the discussion as it flows around you. Be aware of the positive or negative responses that others stimulate in you, and then let these feelings go. Focus on the goal, not the process.

you at that moment. By contrast, meditation requires "single-pointed" attention, in which you focus your mind on one specific word (mantra) or image.

MUSIC AND ATTENTION

Perhaps the quickest and easiest way to change your own level of attention is by using music. The power of rhythmic sound over the brain's activities has been recognized for millennia, and used in activities such as drumming and chanting.

Some scientists think that, as you focus on the rhythm of a piece of music, your brain activity increases or slows down to match.

Choose a selection of your favourite pieces of music to get you into different states of awareness.

- Select exciting, upbeat music to help you shift into top gear.
- Try quiet but complex music (Bach is especially good) to encourage calm, focused concentration.
- Use slow, soothing "chill-out" music to relax and open your mind, for holistic or creative thinking.

INTERLUDE

THE SEEDS OF GENIUS

Intelligence takes many forms, and our view of it has not
remained static – the genius who first worked out how
to create fire from friction would probably not fare well
in a modern IQ test.

ARE WE ALL BECOMING CLEVERER?

It doesn't take a genius to recognize that a roomful
of geniuses will contain a lot more IQ power than a
roomful of people who struggle with basic arithmetic.
But if these two hypothetical groups were set an IQ test
and the results averaged out for each room, most people
in each group would score around 100 – only the value
of 100 in the genius room would be much higher than
the 100 in the so-so room.

This, in effect, is what happens with IQ tests. They
are the average of a particular population at a particular
time. It is generally recognized that, during the time that
IQ has been formally assessed and for which statistics
are available, there has been around a 10-point gain in
IQ with each generation. A number of factors can
account for this, including better nutrition in childhood,
the ironing out of cultural differences inherent in tests
and the changing nature of what and how we learn.
(Comparisons between children taking tests 30 years
ago and now show little difference in numerical or

verbal ability but a notable improvement in spatial and visual abilities, which may relate to skills honed on computer games.)

Inevitably, perhaps, comparisons are made between nations, too. The Japanese appear to top the international IQ league but, like all statistics, international IQ "rankings" need to be taken with a pinch of salt. For example, as the national IQ for Kyrgyzstan is not available, it has been estimated by averaging the IQs of Turkey and Iran!

THE NATURE OF GENIUS

Does having a sky-high IQ make you a genius? Of course it helps, but genius is something more than simply being very clever or talented. It entails a rare ability to see beyond learning, to cross frontiers – the sort of visionary leap that enabled Einstein to formulate the laws governing time and space or Newton to envisage gravity.

Although we've all benefited from the discoveries and inventions of geniuses, the concept of genius also has negative connotations, as a poisoned chalice whose benefits are offset by some huge emotional or social disadvantage. Geniuses are often obsessive, and their clarity of intellectual insight can be depressing and isolating: by nature, geniuses march to a different drum. At least as often as they're hailed as saviours of humankind or brilliant benefactors of society, they're perceived as outsiders, wildly eccentric or mentally troubled – such as Vincent van Gogh or Alan Turing. Mental disturbance can even be a catalyst for genius. That's without mentioning the "mad professors" and "evil geniuses" that populate much of fiction, from Dr Frankenstein to the adversaries of James Bond or Superman.

We need geniuses but each generation may throw up only a few, and they may not be recognized until long after they're dead. Who might be the geniuses among us now?

SECRETS OF THE CURRENT GENIUS POOL

The Canadian psychologist and thinker Elliott Jaques saw intelligence as the capacity to impact on the world around us, and described patterns of influence that span hundreds or thousands of years. Geniuses are exceptional people who have the capacity to influence the direction of human civilization. Here are my suggestions for candidates whom future generations will declare as geniuses.

Hiroshi Ishiguro is a world expert on android robotics. His unique vision is to extend our understanding of humanity by creating a humanity of machines. The ripples of his thinking are likely to evolve into a range of technologies in various fields, such as medicine, where the most complex surgical procedures could be carried out by robots.

Dr Randell Mills is a Harvard-trained medic whose hydrino theory and "blacklight power" could transform power generation. Mills's theory is controversial, but if he is correct, he could liberate the world from the dependency on fossil fuels and nuclear energy, and bring about the greatest single enhancement to the quality of life on Earth.

James Lovelock will forever be associated with the "Gaia" hypothesis: seeing the Earth as a single organism, and recognizing the interdependence of everything in the biosphere, with even the smallest changes potentially having huge ramifications for everything else. His legacy will have been perhaps to evoke an increased sense of personal responsibility in our relationship to the world around us.

Tim Berners-Lee may be the most influential thinker in the last 60 years. His "baby", the Internet, has transformed the world. This completely new form of communication has transcended its original military application to cut through cultural and political barriers, providing a repository of world knowledge and a means of speeding up future technological breakthroughs.

The inspiration of these people can be an example to each of us. In our different ways, we can all use our imaginations as both windows and tools, and we can all find innovative solutions simply by seeing things from a different perspective.

4
APPLIED BRAINPOWER

The skills we use in IQ tests apply to real life too: sharper thinking can help you negotiate your way through a typical day at work or home, whether your activities involve problem-solving, forward planning, creative thinking or grasping the implications of complicated issues.

There are ideas here for applying your increased powers of logical and critical reasoning in different ways, and for exercising that all-important working memory. And because realizing your intellectual potential can give you a real thirst for knowledge, the chapter also offers suggestions on how to build up your resources of information and thus expand your capacity for learning.

YOUR KNOWLEDGE RESERVOIR

Having access to seemingly infinite amounts of information with a few clicks of a computer mouse, do we still need to carry knowledge around in our heads? Should we spend time and effort learning things like facts and figures?

THE VALUE OF KNOWLEDGE

Knowledge isn't intelligence, but developing a rich reservoir of information can confer various advantages in terms of enhancing your overall thinking abilities:

Faster thinking speed

Your mind's retrieval system is far faster than any computer. Having a large knowledge database to draw on instantaneously, speeds up your thoughts and responses.

Deeper comprehension

A broad range of knowledge strengthens your ability to understand complex issues and make decisions. It also increases your ability to see connections between apparently unrelated topics, thus enhancing your capacity for creative thinking.

More efficient memory

A large network of existing knowledge makes it easier for you to learn and remember new information, as explained below.

EXPLOITING THE BRAIN'S STORAGE SYSTEM

The brain has a wonderfully effective storage system that uses a wide variety of tags to retrieve information via associative triggers. We get a glimpse of this process in action with word associations: think bird, think yellow, and immediately CANARY will pop into your mind. All our senses and emotions are involved in this tagging process: a friend's voice conjures up their face in your mind; a whiff of ozone brings to mind a childhood seaside vacation. As we saw on pages 48–9 pathways to and between pieces of information are reinforced by repetition and habit, and by employing more than one of our senses.

This association by multiple stimuli gives us huge potential not only to retrieve material from our memories but to assimilate new information. When we receive data, our brain "files" it with knowledge we already possess, forming associated clusters. So new information is much easier to retain if it relates in some way to something we already know. It's like doing a crossword puzzle – each clue you fill in gives you more help with the remaining answers. School lessons (in theory, at least) are structured to help children's learning in this way, and we use the same process when we're

"Knowledge is the life of the mind."

Abu Bakr (AD 573–634)

adults, whether we're getting to grips with a new job or learning to drive a car. Providing a wealth of "hooks" on which to hang new information increases our learning capability, which is one of the foundations of intelligence.

KNOWLEDGE TREES

A knowledge tree is a visual representation of the main areas and more specialized subjects that make up your personal knowledge database. By drawing one, you can see how much you already know about a topic. You can also use it as a framework to extend and enrich your stores of information.

THE FRAMEWORK OF A KNOWLEDGE TREE

As with a real tree, a knowledge tree has three main parts: the trunk, the branches and the roots.

Trunk This central part represents your overall body of knowledge on a subject. It co-ordinates connections between the different topics and areas of your knowledge.
Branches The branches represent major aspects of your knowledge base. Each one sub-divides into increasingly specific areas.
Roots These take in information from the outside world to nourish the tree. The information might come from other people or organizations; from places, such as libraries; from your own experience; or from media such as books, newspapers, TV, radio and the internet.

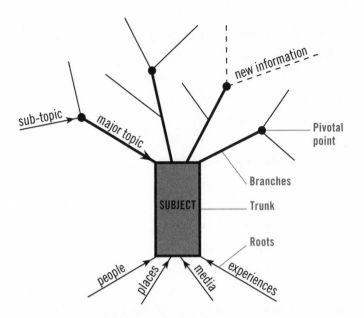

sub-topic — *major topic* — new information –

Pivotal point

Branches

SUBJECT

Trunk

Roots

people — places — media — experiences

WHAT YOUR KNOWLEDGE TREE CAN SHOW

A knowledge tree can help you organize your thoughts on an issue. The branched structure will show you how sub-topics are interrelated, and will encourage you to distinguish the fundamental aspects of a subject from specialized side issues. The tree also shows "pivotal points": junctions that form crucial links to other areas of knowledge, or on which several sub-branches depend.

You can also use your tree as a template to help you build on your stores of knowledge. As we've seen on pages 88–9, we find it easier to absorb new information if we can add it to a pre-existing category or connect it to other facts. The tree will help you to see how new information relates to what you already know, so that your brain can retain it more easily and recall it with less effort. Revisit your tree regularly, and add branches as you update and revise information. The flourishing tree will thus reflect your increasingly detailed and accurate understanding of a subject.

BUILDING YOUR KNOWLEDGE

By adding branches to your knowledge tree, you can reinforce your existing knowledge as well as extending your reach into new areas. The example below shows how to construct and use a tree.

First, choose an area of knowledge on which you'd like to build, and draw branches and sub-branches stemming from this main topic. The example below shows how a wine branch and its sub-branches have grown from the topic of food, but the starting point might equally be a favourite country or a wine-tasting course.

Your smallest sub-branches would indicate specific areas on which you could concentrate. By then learning about, say, a couple of producers in Hawkes Bay, you'd

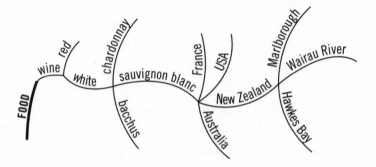

gain an understanding about wine-growing in one area of New Zealand and one varietal grape. However, the new information will also flow back down the bigger branches, feeding other areas of knowledge. Learning about one wine-growing region will add to your knowledge of wine-growing in general, but also to less expected areas, such as geology or climate patterns.

APPLYING YOUR KNOWLEDGE EFFECTIVELY

The "pivotal points" of knowledge, as shown on the diagram on page 91, are the elements on which everything else in a branch of knowledge depends. Feeding the right information through them, or drawing the necessary facts out of them, are the keys to making the most of your knowledge and applying it to best advantage.

For example, if you're a doctor, your knowledge tree might include knowing how to take medical histories from patients, make diagnoses and arrange treatments, but the pivotal point is assessing the patient and carrying out appropriate tests that will give the information needed for accurate diagnosis and the right treatment. Building on a pivotal point can benefit all of the sub-branches leading from that point.

By finding out about a new form of scanning test a doctor might be able to diagnose a whole range of diseases more accurately. In the same way, identifying pivotal points could improve your own work or enable you to learn or research more effectively. Recognizing pivotal points will help you to focus your efforts and resources on "the difference that makes a difference".

Pivotal points are like two-way doors. They are the gateway to new routes of knowledge or advancement, and they are also the point at which new knowledge feeds back into other areas of your overall knowledge tree. For example, you might identify New Zealand's geology as a pivotal point in your wine education: it helps you understand more about the vines grown in Hawkes Bay but could also enable you to see why the wines from other countries with similar geology develop the way they do.

MEMORY ASSOCIATIONS

Building powerful memory associations will stimulate your brain to make strong new neural pathways, and contribute gradually but progressively to the development of your intellectual capacity.

MEMORABLE TECHNIQUES

Many techniques have been devised to help us remember and recall information. What all of these methods do is to add reinforcing sensory or emotional "tags", which, as we saw on pages 89–90, increase our ability to retrieve what our brain has stored. Try different methods, using rhymes, visual images or word associations, to see which works best for you:

BUN FOR 1, SHOE FOR 2

Rhymes are a traditional way to make facts stick in people's minds. To remember number-related facts, start by creating a rhyming list for the numbers 1 to 10. Your list might go as follows:

Bun = 1, **Shoe** = 2, **Tree** = 3, **Boar** = 4, **Dive** = 5 and so on

Choose simple, strong images that have meaning for you, and practise them until you automatically link, say, 6 with "sticks" or 8 with your sister Kate. These images are then ready to help you remember strings of numbers such as telephone numbers or door codes. You can also apply the technique to lists of items in a fixed order. For example, you could create memorable images to learn the periodic table of elements in their correct order:

1 (**Bun**) = hydrogen = a hydrogen bomb like an exploding cream bun
2 (**Shoe**) = helium = shoes so light that wearing them makes you float like a helium balloon
3 (**Tree**) = lithium = a tree sprouting lithium batteries as fruit.

Associating each piece of information with both a visual tag (the image) and an auditory tag (the rhyme) increases its memorability and enables you to retrieve it on demand.

EXPANDING YOUR WORKING MEMORY

Working memory, as we have seen in Chapter 2, is an integral part of thought-processing, and exercising it regularly will contribute to extending your actual IQ.

DIGIT SPANS REVISITED

Remember the test on page 52, when you were asked to memorize a string of numbers – how did you do? That exercise, the Digit Span, might not be very exciting, but it does provide a useful benchmark against which

MEMORY GAMES

Increasing the "reservoir" of your working memory by playing memory games regularly can be fun as well as good mental exercise. Here are some ideas.

Kim's Game This game comes from Rudyard Kipling's book *Kim*. Ask someone to put 15 everyday objects on a tray for you and cover them with a cloth. Then remove the cloth, and allow yourself 30 seconds to scan the objects and commit them to memory. Replace the cloth and try to recall as many objects as you can. Once you can remember 15 objects without error, increase the number of objects or reduce the scanning time. Aim to recall 20 objects after a 15-second scan.

Pelmanism Several people can play this old parlour game. Spread out a deck of cards face down over a table, so that no two overlap. Each player in turn chooses two cards and turns them face up. If the cards are a pair, the player keeps them. If not, they must be turned face down again in the same position. The player who collects the most pairs wins. The first few turns are purely guesswork, but they reveal the position of certain cards. As the game progresses, you'll be able to collect more pairs if you can remember the position of cards you've seen before.

Observation You can practise enhancing your working memory as you go about daily life. While travelling, in a shop or walking around, pause to take a "mental snapshot" of what you can see, then try recalling it a few minutes later. You could focus on specifics, such as people's clothing, where they're sitting, or the layout of objects in a room.

you can measure your capability. Try it a few more times, and work on improving your total. When you can successfully repeat back three different spans of a given length, lengthen the span by an extra digit. With practice you should be able to reach around 15 digits forward and – much more difficult – up to 12 or 13 backwards.

EXPANSION EXERCISES
Mental arithmetic Add up shopping items as they go through the till.

Phone numbers Rehearse them until they're committed to your long-term memory, rather than immediately writing them down or keying them into your phone.

Crosswords Work out anagrams in your head rather than on paper. Try doing a whole crossword in your mind before filling in the squares.

Mental maps Visualize, in detail, the layout of your house; do two- or three-dimensional puzzles. These activities require you to exercise the "visuo-spatial sketch pad" in your working memory (see pp. 50–3).

FORMING OPINIONS

Applying critical analysis isn't a matter of picking holes in your own or others' ideas, but of subjecting them to rational assessment to see them in the clearest light. Learning to view issues in this way can benefit every area of your life.

ELEMENTS OF CRITICAL THINKING

To stay on track, your thinking should have three
main elements:

Correctness Opinions need to be based on accurate
information with as few gaps as possible. Ask yourself:
- What information do I have to support my thinking?
- What information might show it to be false?
- Can I find more details to confirm or refute
  my opinion?

Logic The progression of your thoughts, or their
relationship to each other, needs to make sense.
Ask yourself:
- How do my conclusions follow from my original ideas?
- Are my conclusions deduced from facts or
  assumptions? (See Ladder of inference, p.74.)

Relevance Critical analysis and reasoned debate can
easily be clouded by irrelevancies. Ask yourself:
- How is this thought related to the issue I'm
  considering?
- Will it make any difference if I ignore this point?

EXERCISING YOUR CRITICAL FACULTIES

Practise applying the following types of question,
whether it's to assess the truth of a news story or come
to a reasoned opinion about a book or film. For example:

Responding to a news report:
- What innate bias do I have about the news story that is being reported?
- Am I objecting to/agreeing with the actual views being expressed, or am I being affected by the tone (or even looks) of the reporter?
- Do I know enough to make a judgment yet?

Our background, education and experience can give rise to assumptions or habits of thought that serve well enough in most instances, but these can occasionally cause bias. See pages 67–70 for more information on how such distortions can arise and what you can do to prevent them.

Engaging with a book discussion group:
- What specifically was it about this book that I liked/ didn't enjoy?
- Is my response to the subject, or even to the author, influencing my view of the book's literary merits?
- Have I properly listened and learnt from the opinions of other people?

Egocentricity can make us insufficiently critical of our own ideas and perhaps overly harsh on other people's. Empathy (see p.139) and careful listening (see p.148) will enable you to appreciate other viewpoints, even if you don't agree with them.

INCREASING YOUR POWERS OF LOGIC

Logical, step-by-step reasoning is a key skill in most areas of life. Doing abstract exercises in logic, such as the ones on these pages, will sharpen your reasoning skills, enabling you to assess facts accurately and spot fallacies. The answers to these exercises are on pages 154–6.

SYLLOGISMS

A syllogism is a line of reasoning in which a particular conclusion is inferred from certain premises. As we saw on page 62 with the examples concerning Socrates, not all syllogisms are true.

Consider each of the following syllogisms, and see if you can work out whether it's true or false.

1 All socialists are in favour of higher taxes.
  All elderly people are in favour of higher taxes.
  Therefore, all elderly people are socialists.

2 All mammals are warm-blooded.
  All whales are mammals.
  Therefore, all whales are warm-blooded.

"Fix reason firmly in her seat, and call to her tribunal every fact, every opinion."

Thomas Jefferson (1743–1826)

3 All swans are white.
This bird is black.
Therefore, this bird cannot be a swan.

FALLACIES

A fallacy is a line of reasoning that seems correct at first glance, but actually contains mistakes that can easily go unnoticed. Can you identify what's wrong with the following? When you've read the answers, try to think of other examples of the same types of fallacy.

4 Joe's Hamburger Joint opened in 2005. The number of rats in the neighbourhood has fallen since 2005. I suspect Joe's Hamburger Joint has caused mass fatality in rats.

5 Why are women so obsessed with shopping?

6 Since nobody has ever proven that life doesn't exist on any other planets in the universe, we can safely assume that aliens are out there somewhere.

7 We should be kind to one another. Einstein said so, and he was one of the most brilliant men who ever lived.

8 Mark says his team won their last football match by 4–1, but Lee says they won by 2–1; therefore the team must have won by 3–1.

CORRECTING ERRORS IN REASONING

In Chapter 3, we saw how subconscious beliefs and faulty reasoning can lead to muddled or wrong thinking. The inference chain, shown below, can help you to identify and counteract such biases.

THE INFERENCE CHAIN

The ladder of inference shown on page 74 is only part of the process by which we form opinions. When coming to conclusions, we should check inferences and conclusions against the facts – but that doesn't always happen. Instead, some of our conclusions, whether right or wrong, can become entrenched as beliefs. We then look for selective details to back up these beliefs, and use the details as a basis for further inferences and assumptions, bypassing observable facts. If we don't test each link in the chain, we can make errors of judgment – as in the little story on the following page.

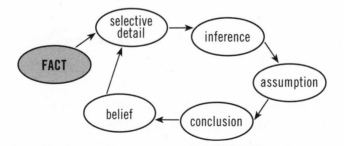

THE INFERENCE CHAIN AT WORK

Imagine the following scenario:

Event 1: You see a tattooed young man strutting down the street. He pauses and stares across the road at an older man.

Assumption 1: Young men can be dangerous; tattooed men are really dangerous. This thought is based on a selective detail: his tattoos.

Assumption 2: The older man is carrying a briefcase; he's probably a businessman. Another supposition has arisen from a selective detail.

Event 2: The young man looks from side to side (seeming very shifty), then dashes across the road and pushes the businessman hard.

Interpretation: The thug is going to rob the man.

Action/conclusion: It seems you were right. But then …

Event 3: A truck is rolling backward down the road, with nobody in it. By pushing the older man, the "thug" has got him out of the way.

Reinterpretation: The young man has saved the older one's life – he's a hero, not a thug!

Event 4: The briefcase spills expensive jewellery over the road and the police arrive on the scene.

Another reinterpretation needed: The older man has just

robbed a store; the briefcase isn't the sign of respectability that you assumed.

This scenario shows how repeated questioning and realigning of your views can prevent fallacious reasoning from going too far. You can also use the sequence in the inference chain backwards, by taking something you believe to be true and checking the validity of each stage on which it was built.

SOLVING PROBLEMS INTELLIGENTLY

The ability to overcome a problem depends on two factors: an accurate perception of the issue and a well-planned course of steps toward a solution.

A MULTI-LAYERED STRATEGY

When struggling with a problem, try breaking it down so that you can work through each stage logically.

Level 1: Define the problem What exactly is the problem? Why is it a problem?
Level 2: Determine the extent of the problem See overleaf
Level 3: Clarify goals What steps must I take to reach the solution?
Level 4: Generate options How many options do I have? What are the possible outcomes for each?
Level 5: Gather feedback How can I test my chosen

A PROBLEM FISH

Problems seldom spring fully formed out of the blue – they usually result from a combination of causes that feed into events or other aspects, which, in turn, build up to form the overall situation.

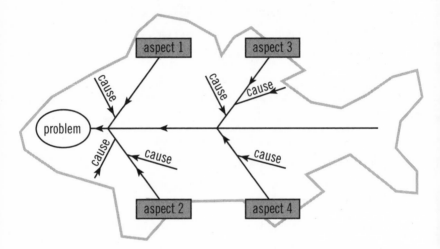

When you've defined your problem, identify the main aspects (people, resources, events, and so on). Look for as many causes as possible (no matter how unlikely) for each aspect. Questions that may help include:

- How many areas does the problem affect?
- When does it occur – all the time, or only at specific times?
- Why is this specific factor a cause?

The result may highlight a pivotal point (see p.91) which, once resolved, clears the entire problem, or show steps toward a solution.

options quickly and easily? Whom can I consult for further information or guidance?

Level 6: Take action!

FISHING FOR CAUSES ...

The "fishbone" diagram opposite is a helpful way to work out the causes of a problem. Your problem forms the head of the "fish". From it draw a horizontal line, with diagonal "bones" branching off it to represent the main aspects. Label each line. For each aspect, consider possible causes and write these in as smaller "bones".

STRATEGIC THINKING

Strategy is the use of planning or foresight to achieve a longer-term objective. It can help you to use your intelligence in a more proactive way.

SUN TZU AND *THE ART OF WAR*

The Chinese general Sun Tzu wrote *The Art of War*, in the 6th century BC, which describes a host of approaches to achieving goals without necessarily engaging in combat. Some of his sayings are perfect examples of attributes of intelligence covered in this book: forward planning, flexible thinking and understanding other people. Here are some direct quotes and how to apply the advice.

There are not more than five primary colours (blue, yellow, red, white and black), yet in combination they produce more hues than can ever be seen.

There are no limits to your capacity to be innovative in your thinking, and no limits to the resources that your creativity can unlock.

The control of a large force is the same principle as the control of a few men: it is merely a question of dividing up their numbers.

To get to grips with a big problem, break it down. Complex problems can always be reduced to key issues, and tasks separated into smaller, more manageable stages.

Do not rely not on the likelihood of the enemy's not coming, but on our own readiness to receive him; not on the chance of his not attacking, but rather on the fact that we have made our position unassailable.

There is no substitute for informed decision-making. The more clearly and accurately you can appraise a situation, and the more carefully you plan your response to it, the more likely you are to be successful.

Military tactics are like unto water, which in its natural course runs from high places and hastens downwards.

This statement emphasizes the need to take the path of least resistance. It's a sound philosophy that allows you to work to your strengths and to avoid what is difficult or unrewarding.

Just as water retains no constant shape, so in warfare there are no constant conditions.

You need to accept that life inevitably involves change. To stay ahead of the game, you need to be flexible and constantly on the lookout for changes in your situation.

The general, unable to control his irritation, will launch his men to the assault like swarming ants, with the result that one-third of his men are slain, while the town still remains untaken.

Understanding your emotions is likely to help you to make objective choices and to avoid irrational decisions that might be driven by the need to avoid, defeat or dominate.

5
SMART
THINKING

There's a well-used saying: "It's not what you've got, it's what you do with it." There are plenty of intelligent people who are not very smart — they have the intellectual capability to understand or do something, but perhaps may not see its potential applications, or may not be good at unlocking complex issues to reveal simple ideas and solutions. Real intelligence involves thinking smarter, not necessarily harder, and recognizing the value of adapting what has been learnt in one field to speed progress in another.

HARDER OR SMARTER?

Working hard has traditionally been viewed as a positive virtue, but it has its downside. Seeking easier or more efficient approaches or solutions to issues is all part of using your intelligence to its full.

THE VIRTUE OF HARD WORK?

People are often praised for working hard, and a good result achieved without effort can be seen as somehow less "worthy" than a similar outcome achieved by hard work. But does this always make sense? Nobody would think it commendable to drive via C and D and E just to get from A to B, or to scrub laundry in the river when you have a washing machine. Yet in thinking, we often toil along familiar routes, overlooking options that might yield greater rewards from less effort. Excessively hard work tires the brain and blunts our thinking ability. Piling effort on effort can cause a build-up of stress and problems such as depression, anxiety and panic attacks.

THE DANGERS OF OVERWORK
In many works of literature and folk stories, the moral is that hard work brings rewards. However, George Orwell's classic satirical novel *Animal Farm* sounds a warning note about over-exertion. Boxer the cart-horse works more than any other animal: his constant motto is, "I will work harder." Finally he collapses – and his cruel masters, the pigs, then sell him for slaughter. Boxer's sad story reminds us that it's important to work smarter, not just harder, if your efforts are not to be wasted.

A careful, step-by-step approach can be appropriate in some situations, such as when you are going through accounts. But the beauty of the brain is that it is capable of flying.

As an example, a birdwatcher wouldn't laboriously check every feature of the birds he sees darting around him – instead, he'd draw on his experience to make an instant guess about each bird's identity, then check a few salient points. His mind needs to be as quick, agile and free-flying as the birds.

LIGHTNING CALCULATIONS

Mental arithmetic provides many examples of smart routes that save time and effort. Here are just two:

Multiplication When multiplying, for example, 24 x 8, it's quicker and easier to calculate 25 x 8 = 200, then subtract 8 to reach 192.

Addition To add up all of the numbers between 1 and 20, you don't need to add 1 + 2 + 3 + 4 ... up to 20. Because 1 + 20 = 21, 2 + 19 = 21, and so on, and there are ten of these pairs of numbers, you just need to do one sum, 21 x 10, to find the total.

SKIM-READING

The ability to skim-read can help you quickly and easily pick out just what you need from a piece of text. Instead of reading each line on a page and saying the words in your mind, let your eyes zig-zag down a whole page at a glance. To check that you've got the sense of the text, jot down key words and phrases straight afterwards. Then re-read the page more slowly to see if you're correct. With practice, you'll be able to take in more information at each attempt.

HOW DO YOU WORK?

A good starting point for assessing your appetite for smart options is to look at your view of work. Do you relish or shrink from challenges? Do you work harder than necessary, or do you under-perform? Your attitude to challenges and to effort provides the motive force for your working style.

CHALLENGES

Our instinctive response to challenges, whether physical (such as a raging bull) or mental (such as a pile of incomprehensible legal paperwork), arises from ancient survival instincts embedded in the deepest part of our brain (see pp.136–8). These instincts can cause us to react in one of three ways:

Fight We attack the problem with a I will "never-be-beaten" attitude.

Flight We try to avoid the problem, or even pass it on to someone else.

Freeze We feel overwhelmed and defeated, and then we surrender.

The easiest, smartest way to cope with challenges is to get yourself into the "flow" state (see p.61), in which your mind has enough stimulation to work effectively but not so much that you panic.

If you find yourself getting stressed, do a few minutes' physical activity – stretch your limbs, take a walk, do a household chore. This will burn off the nervous energy that gives rise to "fight" or "flight" reactions; it can also nudge you out of a panicky "freeze" state.

EFFORT

Do you work late several times a week, or skip off early as often as possible? If someone asks you to do something, do you immediately say yes? The "Protestant work ethic", or a similarly moralistic view of the virtues of hard work, is deeply ingrained in many people. Conversely, other people sabotage their own efforts by not exerting themselves to do their best. How would you best describe your own approach to work: dedicated, moderate or relaxed?

If you're highly dedicated, you might take on more work than is strictly necessary. You might ignore simpler solutions because these take the sweat out of

"If I have seen further it is by standing on the shoulders of giants."

Isaac Newton (1642–1727)

achievement and so "don't feel right". If you habitually do just as much as a job needs, but no more – or if you prefer to take the easy way through life – you might enjoy a comfortable existence, but may never know the thrill of finding out just what you're capable of.

Working "smart" involves all three approaches. Moderate effort should be enough for most everyday tasks. Sometimes you need to take things easy in order to refresh your mind, or to let your subconscious get to work on a knotty problem. But occasionally you may need to stretch yourself to the maximum. Assess your natural attitude and learn to recognize when a different approach is required.

FOUR-STRAND ANALYSIS

Whether it's figuring out who's right in a political argument or studying Chinese history, mastering a complex subject usually involves assimilating a huge variety of factors. A useful tool for untangling such multi-faceted issues is a four-stranded form of analysis called PEST.

THE BASIS OF PEST

PEST is an acronym that stands for

Political   Economic   Sociocultural   Technical

PEST is usually applied to large-scale issues, from pollution to poverty and climate change. On a personal level, this system can enable you to analyze complex issues in depth and from different angles. It will help you to put your facts and opinions into context, so that you can make sense of often conflicting information. As a result, it will enable you to clarify your own thinking and argue from a position of strength.

THE BENEFITS OF PEST
- Unravels the different strands of a complex topic
- Helps you to understand the deeper impact of an issue
- Helps you to capitalize on opportunities and identify any problems
- Encourages you to think of the reasoning behind and the consequences of your stance on any issue.

PEST AT WORK
Consider a complex issue in the light of each PEST component in turn. Here's how it might work when applied to the topic of nuclear power.

Political factors
You might ask yourself: What is government policy on nuclear power? Has it changed? Is the policy different in other countries? Who are the main pressure groups, and what are their stances, pro and con?

Economic factors

Energy choices involve two financial elements: start-up costs and continuing provision. You could look into the costs of different fuels in the short term and long term, for providers and consumers.

Sociocultural factors

How power is generated has social implications, not least in terms of employment and environmental impact. You might also find out more about the repercussions if any source of power became unavailable.

Technical factors

The technicalities of turning any source of fuel into consumable power are complicated but a satisfyingly meaty subject to master. You might call on the help of other mind tools to help you study.

Once you've tackled the issue strand by strand like this, you should find it easier to bring the strands together into a cohesive whole.

SIX HATS THINKING

Edward de Bono developed the Six Hats technique to help people broaden their perspectives on any issue. Without this framework, de Bono believes, we rely on only one or two of the "hats" he describes, leaving a huge hole in the thinking that could potentially be applied to an issue.

Blue Hat (sky)	The big picture, the overview
Red Hat (fire)	Emotions, intuition and feelings
Yellow Hat (sun)	Positive thinking, praise and reasons why something will work
Green Hat (plant)	Creative thinking, where everything goes and nothing is censored
White Hat (blank sheet)	Purely the facts, figures and details
Black Hat (judge's robe)	Critical thinking, judgment and the negatives – why something won't work

WHAT ARE THE SIX HATS?

De Bono identified six key forms of thinking, and characterized them as different hats, each associated with a specific colour and image. The Six Hats technique takes the idea of "putting on your thinking cap" one step further. By mentally "putting on" a hat of a particular colour, you apply the associated mode of thought to an issue. This strategy is designed to jerk you out of your habitual tracks of thinking. The six hats, and their characteristics, are summarized below.

THE BENEFITS OF SIX HATS THINKING

- Diversifies thinking, enabling you to think "out of the box"
- Helps you to broaden your view of an issue
- Enables clearer, faster decision-making

- If used in discussions: provides a structure, promotes interesting views, frees up contributors' thinking and boosts confidence.

MAKING IT WORK

To work on a problem or think about an issue, wear your "hats" in the following order:

- **Blue** to set out an agenda and to map out the extent of the topic.
- **Red** to flush out the emotional dimensions. Consider honestly your true feelings and motives, without analyzing the ramifications. In a meeting, having people don their "red hats" allows them to wear their hearts on their sleeves, making their communication more transparent; it also shifts the issues away from the personal to the collective.
- **Yellow** to look at the benefits and the payoffs of a choice, or the positive aspects of an argument.
- **Green** to generate all the options that may be available.
- Finally, alternate **White** and **Black** to get the solution finely tuned.

As you change from hat to hat, take care to re-focus your thinking each time, to match the colour and features of the new hat you've "put on".

By doing this, you will be able to keep your mind open and avoid falling into any unhelpful habits of thought.

THE BOSTON MATRIX

We usually think of business and personal life as being distinct, but often lessons learnt in one area can benefit the other. The four-way matrix, also called the "Boston matrix", is a business strategy tool that you can adapt to promote clear and logical thinking.

A FOUR-WAY MATRIX

This matrix, the brain-child of Bruce Henderson for the Boston Consulting Group, provides companies with an intelligence tool to help them map out their marketing strategy, and to focus their efforts and resources efficiently. Below is a simplified form of the matrix.

Star Exciting new concept: needs extra resources but gives high returns	**Problem child** Developing concept: needs high input but could give high returns
Cash cow Reliable oldie: needs little input but gives healthy returns	**Dodo** Concept past its sell-by date: might need to be abandoned

BENEFITS OF THE MATRIX

- Helps you to clarify the costs and benefits of the different options
- Encourages you to override emotional attachment to inefficient, "no-win" options, and to cut your losses
- Can be used repeatedly to track changes over time.

ADAPTING THE MATRIX FOR YOURSELF

According to the four-way matrix, it's best for businesses to have a combination of stars to provide new energy, cash cows to keep a steady stream of resources flowing in, and problem children, with the potential to become stars. The same thinking can apply to personal situations: you need a mixture of goals to aim for, untried possibilities to stretch your thinking, and a comfort zone as a secure foundation.

Draw up your own version of the matrix shown below. Allow plenty of room for writing notes in each box.

Goal/Solution	Untried Possibility
Comfort Zone	Dead Duck/Starting Point

Perhaps you know your goal, but not how to get there. In the bottom right-hand box, set out where you're starting from, and in the top left-hand box write your goal. Next, list all the possible solutions you can think of, then locate each of these options in the two remaining boxes. For example, a way-out idea that comes close to your goal would be an Untried Possibility but lie near the Goal/Solution box; an option that gives only a tiny step forward would be low down in the Comfort Zone.

Alternatively, you could use the matrix if you have ideas buzzing about in your brain but no specific goal. As before, write the ideas in the relevant boxes, and relative to the other boxes. The juxtapositions you create might reveal a fresh chain of thought or course of action.

MANAGING INFORMATION

While the brain has an incredible capacity for new information, invariably there are limitations. One of the smart things to learn is the way to distinguish between what you need to know and what you need to find out.

KNOWING WHAT YOU NEED TO KNOW

In the age of the information superhighway, trying to learn everything indiscriminately is pointless. A different way of acquiring knowledge is not to store it in your own memory, but to have reliable, up-to-date sources of information at your fingertips. Those in professions such as the law or finance have long been aware that their efficacy lies not in the sheer weight of what they know, but in their ability to ask the right questions and know where to go for *appropriate* answers.

That emphasis on *appropriate* is important, because with so much information available from so many sources, one of the vital uses of intelligence is to sort the wheat from the chaff. Ten minutes surfing the net, or an hour or so scanning newspapers, will turn up a lot of shaky factoids presented as concrete fact – and, as we've already found (see pp. 73–4), it's very easy to build on false assumptions.

In seeking out and assessing information sources you'll inevitably absorb some of their content, thereby enriching your inbuilt database of knowledge. But, more importantly, you'll be using your critical faculties and organizational abilities to provide yourself with rapid access to valid, reliable information: a smart use of your intelligence.

SOURCING INFORMATION

American psychologist Urie Bronfenbrenner developed a system for ranking the elements of a person's environment from personal to global, each element "nested" within the next like a stack of bowls. This structure can be adapted for organizing sources of information on a subject or family of subjects – anything from Shakespeare's plays to technical developments at work. An example of nested sources that you might utilize in your job is shown below.

1 microsystem (personal level)
2 mesosystem (interaction of two microsystems)
3 exosystem (direct external influences)
4 macrosystem (wider social and cultural environment)
5 chronosystem (a set of external systems that extend and evolve over time)

Examples of sources

1 Local clubs or interest groups; personal experience or networks
2 Further training or personal development courses; local and regional government organizations
3 Professional and trade websites and journals
4 General print and broadcast media; web-based encyclopedias
5 Government and global sources, such as the United Nations.

DEVELOPING KNOWLEDGE ROOTS

Setting up your framework of sources will take time and critical thought, but will prove an effective use of time and brainpower.

Stage 1

• Evaluate promising sources and sort them into different categories.
• Aim to include sources from all levels (see opposite). Seek breadth and variety of information: for example,

"Knowledge is of two kinds: we know a subject ourselves, or we know where we can find information upon it."

Samuel Johnson (1709–84)

LIFE HACKING

Life hacking is the art of solving life's problems using shortcuts and clever solutions. It began in the techno-world of computers but has developed quite a momentum, with websites dedicated to sharing and evolving life-hacking solutions such as how to get your email inbox to zero, smart ways to study and how to cope with information overload.

Find the best way for you Save time and effort by learning, analyzing or memorizing in the way that suits you best. Don't struggle with Mind Maps® if you're a natural list-maker; don't feel obliged to play music while you work just because you've heard that Mozart encourages genius.

Release your mind from minutiae Nagging small thoughts that demand your attention prevent you from giving time to clear thinking, planning and learning. Writing things down as they occur to you will release your mind from clutter, but prevent you from forgetting the little things.

Choose your targets carefully Life-hackers take "to-do" lists a stage further by looking for common factors that can enable them to do one or more tasks in a single action. Apply this to your intellectual development, too. See pages 90–4 to find out how knowledge trees can help you identify pivotal points to maximize learning or action.

Measure twice, cut once This traditional craftsman's saying highlights the need to work out a clear plan of action before tackling a task, so that you can get the job done quickly and efficiently.

look at newspapers that you wouldn't usually read, or tune in to a radio station that isn't one of your usual choices.

Stage 2
- Establish access to sources that update themselves regularly (such as subscribing to newsletters, journals, clubs or societies).
- Add useful websites to your favourites list.

Stage 3
- Watch out for new information sources to add to your framework.
- Factor in adequate time to review and consolidate any new information.

ADAPTABILITY

Smart people recognize that flexibility in thinking is a vital asset to be nurtured and exercised. We need adaptability to survive in our fast-moving world, and responding to change can sometimes turn even crises into golden opportunities.

CHANGE HAPPENS

However orderly and rational our thinking may be, we need to be able to cope with change in whatever form it appears. And changes don't come only from outside, in the form of altered circumstances or the actions or influences of other people – they can emanate from within ourselves, too, as we add to our knowledge and our experience.

You can ignore or avoid change, try to dominate it by strength of will, or accept it, like a tree bending with every passing breeze. But these are just short-term fixes: they won't enable you to expand your mind by responding positively to change and learning from it.

PROCESSES OF CHANGE

To handle changes, it helps to know how they can arise. Certain change processes have been identified in science, economics and sociology, but you can also see them at work in daily life. They include:

Diminishing returns This law of economics states that if one type of input into a product is increased while others stay fixed, after a certain point there will be ever smaller increases in output. For example, doubling the number of cows in a field does not automatically double the milk yield, because an overcrowded pasture will diminish the milk yield from each cow.

Feedback loop When one change causes a further change, the result feeds back and accelerates or limits the rate of change. Climate change is an example of an accelerating change. As the Earth warms, the polar icecaps start to melt and there is less ice to reflect heat away from the Earth's surface, so warming increases.

Tipping point Small or slow changes may individually seem of little consequence but cumulatively their effect can tip the balance over the point of no return. For example, when tourists start buying up houses in a popular holiday area, at a certain point regular residents may start leaving in significant numbers, causing the character of the location to alter quickly. If a species population drops below a viable number, extinction will become hard to avoid.

Network effect As an idea is taken up, its spread accelerates. Cell phones, for example, only started to become widespread once the number of phones in use, and the extent of the networks, grew large enough to make the idea appealing.

MENTAL FLEXIBILITY

How we view change, whether it's self-imposed or thrust upon us, depends on our mental agility, because change involves absorbing new information, formulating fresh ideas and perhaps changing focus or viewpoint. Becoming adept at these skills will keep you ahead of the game at work, prevent your mind from getting stuck in a rut as you get older and enable you to embrace rather than resist change when you have to face it. Remember the martial arts principle that an opponent's weight or strength can be turned to your advantage.

One way to stay flexible and ready for change is to create actual challenges for yourself all the time. However, this is not always realistic or even a good idea – a case of making unnecessary work. But, as we have seen, applying knowledge learnt in one field to other areas is good use of intelligence. So, seek out mental exercises that test your agility and demand adaptability. Here are a few ideas.

- Join a debating society (or create a group with friends) where the emphasis is on the quality of the argument – a good debater can put the case for both sides with equal conviction.
- Have a go at approaching word puzzles from the other direction – make up your own crossword puzzle or devise a fiendish code for your children to break.
- Set yourself a sequence of short but very different tasks – for example, helping with science homework, and then reading a French novel – to practise rapid changes in thinking modes.
- Play board games that have an element of chance: these games force players to rethink their strategy all the time.

TEN QUESTIONS SMART PEOPLE KEEP ASKING

To work through an issue, repeatedly ask yourself some or all of the following smart questions. Searching for the answers can help you to keep on track in many different situations, from historical research or scientific study to considering your career path.

- Who's already trodden this path and could help me?
  - Am I coming at this from the right angle?
    - Am I over-complicating this?
    - Am I over-simplifying this?
  - What avenues does this information open up?
  - What avenues does this information close down?
    - What can I learn from this?
      - Is this true?
      - Is this *still* true?

      and, of course:

      - **Why?**

"Judge a man by his questions, rather than by his answers."

Voltaire (1694–1778)

HAVING FUN

One of the privileges of adult life is not having to study formally or undergo exams unless we choose to. This can allow us to expand our knowledge and apply our intelligence in any way we wish – including just for fun.

LETTING YOUR MIND OUT TO PLAY

Because we learn through practice and experience, we can use virtual challenges as a way to rehearse our skills in reasoning, problem-solving, flexibility and strategic thinking. Puzzles and games are an ideal source of such challenges: as well as entertaining us, they can make us better prepared for thinking flexibly when actual life demands it. So enjoy board games (or their online equivalent, fantasy gaming) – look upon them as a form of subconscious mental training.

BRAIN-TEASERS

Jokes and riddles are another way to enjoy stretching your mental powers. By showing a funny or unexpected view of the world, or by exposing fallacies in your reasoning, they encourage you to "think outside the box". You might like to try the following examples; the answers are at the bottom of the page opposite.

1 A woman went into a DIY store. She found the items she wanted, but needed to find out the prices. She asked the shop assistant, "How much does one cost?"

"Two dollars," replied the assistant.

"How much would 14 cost?" the customer inquired.

"Four dollars," came the reply.

"So how much would 144 cost?" the customer wanted to know.

"Six dollars," she was told.

What was the woman buying?

2 Imagine you have a round fruit cake – how would you divide it into eight equal pieces by making only three cuts?

3 How many letters are there in the alphabet?

4 I walked into a party and the room was full of people – yet I didn't see one single person. Why not?

Answers:

1 She was buying numbers to put on the front door of her house.

2 First slice the cake in half horizontally, parallel to the plate, then cut it into quarters in the normal way.

3 There are 11 letters in "the alphabet".

4 Everyone in the room was married.

6
REALIZING YOUR ASSETS

Overall intelligence involves an awareness of feelings and instincts as well as the use of logical, analytical skills. Even rare individuals whose exceptional mental skills and high IQ set them apart from ordinary people – top mathematicians and scientists, for example – expand and enhance their abilities by drawing on the less obvious or measurable aspects of intelligence. By understanding the non-rational aspects of your psychology, you can create for yourself an environment in which your intelligence can flourish.

This final chapter also explores the ongoing development of your intellectual capacity: how you can generate new ideas to complement your new take on the world, how to give and receive help from others and how to benefit from the enriched intellectual ability you can continue to bring to your life.

REASON AND EMOTION

Our mind is constantly assessing and responding to our ever-changing environment. This subtle, continuous activity is made possible by our emotions and reasoning processes, which have evolved over millions of years.

OUR THREE-IN-ONE BRAIN

In the 1970s, neurologist Paul MacLean came up with the theory that our brain has a "triune" (three-in-one) structure, which he associated with the main stages of human evolution: from reptile to mammal and then to our present form. Each of the three layers has specific functions, but all three interact with each other.

Reptilian brain

The brain stem and cerebellum are the most ancient in evolutionary terms. In reptiles, they form the largest part of the brain. In humans, the reptilian brain controls the automatic functions that keep us alive, such as

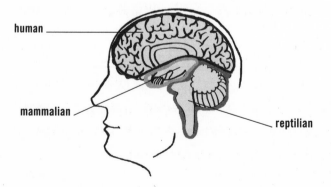

human

mammalian

reptilian

breathing and heartbeat. It also governs basic survival behaviour, which is hard-wired into us and very difficult to change.

Mammalian brain

This part of the brain has evolved in mammals, including humans, to govern memory and the expression of emotions. Unlike the automatic reflexes of the reptilian brain, the mammalian brain enables us to adapt our responses to cope with changing situations. It helps us to make value judgments ("this food is nice"; "that person is horrid"), pay attention to important things, and prioritize. However, strong reactions from this part of our brain can sometimes cause biases or other distortions in our thinking.

Human brain

The cerebral cortex, the part we recognize most readily in pictures of the brain, is the largest and most dominant area in primates and particularly in humans. This controls IQ-related functions such as language, reasoning, forward planning, abstract thought and creativity. It also enables us to interpret our feelings, and to come up with sophisticated responses to situations.

Although this outermost layer of our brain controls our most human attributes, it is still influenced by the more primitive areas and can't function effectively without them. In fact, a very dense network of nerves connects the human and mammalian layers, which indicates the powerful role of emotions in our thought processes.

EMOTIONAL INTELLIGENCE

Intelligence is much more than the sum of our IQ skills. One concept reflecting this broader view is that of "emotional intelligence": a blend of thought and emotion, which involves empathy as well as knowledge, and draws on feeling and instinct as well as reasoning.

THE ESSENCE OF EMOTIONAL INTELLIGENCE

Clever people sometimes do stupid things: they might lose their tempers with colleagues, or storm out of a meeting because of frustration. Conversely, some people who might not be considered highly intelligent can be much more wise about other people and skilled at handling situations. So what makes the difference?

The answer is emotional intelligence. Psychologist and author Daniel Goleman, who popularized this term, defined it as the master aptitude that enables us to use our other thinking skills successfully. It has also been associated with "interpersonal" and "intrapersonal" intelligence, two of the "multiple intelligences" defined by Harvard psychologist Howard Gardner. Emotional intelligence has to do with our ability to regulate our own non-rational feelings, and to interpret other people's emotions accurately. The main elements are:

Self-awareness This is the ability to recognize one's own emotions as they are happening, and to identify their causes. It is also what prevents us from becoming overwhelmed by strong feelings such as excitement, fear or anger. Self-awareness is what stops us from being misled by optimism or, conversely, crippled by pessimism, and it helps us to be able to perceive situations more accurately.

Emotional control The ability to express feelings appropriately and regulate unhelpful feelings. It enables us to practise self-discipline, motivate ourselves and tolerate frustration, which, in turn, helps us to maintain clarity and balance in our thinking.

Empathy The ability to "read" other people's expressions and actions, and work out what they want or need. It may seem as though empathy has little to do with IQ skills, but of course most of the issues in our lives involve other people, so being able to understand others or even predict how they might act will help you to achieve your own aims.

As you develop your intelligence, you'll need to match your improvements in reasoning with an increased skill at managing your emotions and dealing with the reactions of others, to enable you to achieve the maximum expression of your thinking capacity.

TAMING THE BEASTS

The archaic responses we retain from our primitive past
are not always helpful in the modern world. For example,
the reptilian brain's survival instincts tend to follow
unvarying response patterns, and these can become even
more fixed when we're under stress, leading to obsessive
behaviour or repetitive cycles.

Similarly, animal emotions can sometimes hijack
human reason and judgment. An obvious example is
the way in which worrying can interfere with your
thinking as you're working, studying – or even doing
an IQ test. It pushes you beyond your ideal "flow" state
(see pp. 59–61) into a panic zone where your memory
and reasoning skills desert you. As a result, you're more
likely to make a mistake, which then causes you to feel
bad and dread having to do similar tasks in the future.
Conversely, feeling happy, positive or relaxed frees up
your thinking and, for example, encourages you to
explore more adventurous solutions to problems.

But the instinctual and emotional parts of our make-
up are what make us human, so they can't and shouldn't
be ignored or straitjacketed. Harmonizing reason and
emotion is the essence of emotional intelligence. It can

*"All of our reasoning ends in surrender
to feeling."*

Blaise Pascal (1623–62)

help us to avoid being paralyzed by angst about the past or fear for the future. It can also help us to avoid or short-circuit distorted patterns of thinking (see The Inference Chain, p.103).

We can perform this transformation by, for example, working through steps from rage to positive action: first by recognizing the emotion that is underlying our instinctual reactions, then rationalizing and putting it into context, then seeing the source of negative feeling as a problem to be solved rather than a threat to be fought.

ENHANCED IQ IN PRACTICE

Enhancing your intellectual ability is rather like becoming incredibly fit – effort seems effortless and you can take on new challenges with extra confidence. This change may take you by surprise, and you may think and behave in such a different way that other people notice, too.

PERSONAL POTENTIAL

Greater sharpness and clarity of thinking, and an ability to unravel complexities, will give you an appetite for learning more and rising to challenges. To realize your potential fully, you need to:
- Discover how to make the most of your intellectual and personal capacities
- Develop an ability to see the bigger picture

- Develop a related capacity: looking into the future to see which seeds of ideas and plans show the greatest promise.

A combination of new knowledge, increased adaptability and greater powers of critical analysis allows you to evaluate information from all sources in a broader and more informed way. You'll feel benefits from your enhanced IQ having an impact on your life in general, such as:

- A better grasp of current affairs
- Sharper, more efficient approaches to tasks or learning at work
- Pleasure in testing your abilities in ever-harder mental tests
- A desire to return to study.

Your enquiring mind may develop in an obvious direction – perhaps research at work or getting to grips with subjects in which you had previously floundered, such as economics or politics – but it can also open up completely new directions for you.

NEW IDEAS

Nowadays you don't need to have face-to-face access to the great minds of academe or those at the cutting edge to share their findings and discuss ideas with like-minded people. Try feeding your mind through previously untapped sources, such as internet blogs and chatrooms for a particular interest you wish to explore.

Applying your intelligence often involves coming at an issue from a whole new angle. Use your creative, right-brain thinking or look for themes in one area of knowledge that you can import into other areas. This is how many inventions and breakthroughs are triggered, from the Apple iPhone® to peace in a war-torn country.

LOOKING TO THE FUTURE

Having come this far, you might have reached a point where you ask yourself the question "What next?" This is your chance to take a breathing space, then review how far you've come and consider what your future direction might be.

THE WHEEL OF PROGRESS

The wheel below is a tool that you can use to chart your progress in improving your IQ skills. The segments represent the key elements of IQ enhancement explored in this book so far. The rings represent the levels of improvement, with the central ring standing for the lowest level and the outermost ring signifying the highest level.

Draw your own wheel and, taking each "pie section" in turn, mark where you think that you are in terms of your current strengths and weaknesses. For example, if you feel you've made little progress in sorting out distortions in your thinking, you might only colour in or "award" yourself the innermost segment for that section. If you see significant improvements with, say, building knowledge and managing information, you'd colour in perhaps four or five segments. You can use this wheel again to check progress in three months' time.

1   IQ test scores
2   Thinking/reaction speed
3   Nutrition/physical health
4   Straight thinking
5   Working memory
6   Logic and reasoning
7   Increasing knowledge
8   Smart thinking

MAKING A LIFE PLAN

People who achieve what they want usually follow a clear plan: they carefully map out what they want to happen, and then do things that turn their plan into reality. They take certain courses or learn certain skills. They join associations and network with like-minded people. They learn to think their way to achieving what they want.

Similarly, by drawing up your own life plan, you can define the ways in which you wish to improve your IQ and set goals for applying your enhanced intelligence in all areas of your life. As you follow your plan, you'll recognize in yourself a broadening of horizons – whether in work, academic studies, leisure, or simply being able to understand the world from a more enlightened angle.

The page overleaf suggest how to construct a three-month plan. Your life plan should include definite goals for personal development: you can use the Boston matrix (see p.121) or four-strand analysis (see p.116) to help you determine key development areas. The plan should also include activities that will enrich every day. Whatever you choose, your IQ programme as a whole should fit into the big picture that you have for your life.

GETTING HELP FROM OTHERS

Virtually everything we do involves interactions with other people. We often neglect to draw on others' knowledge and experience, but their support can greatly help us in our quest to realize our intellectual potential.

A THREE-MONTH PLAN

You can make plans as far into the future as you like, but most of
the improvements described in this book are achievable in
a fairly short time. Three months should be a manageable period
– long enough to make noticeable advances but short enough
not to be daunting.

Set clear goals Define each goal in one brief sentence. Frame it
using positive rather than negative words: "I will increase my IQ
scores," for example, rather than "I won't go to pieces in exams."

Keep track of your progress Refer to your progress wheel
(see p.144). Set yourself specific goals in each sector: for example,
"improve digit span by three numbers" (see pp.96–8) for sector 5,
or "add a new element to my fitness regime" for sector 3. Tackle
your weakest sectors first, and try to raise your levels there; this will
give the biggest boost to your overall brain improvement.

Build in variety Keep your mind fresh by having a mixture
of quick, easy tasks (such as doing a crossword or a logic puzzle
every day) and larger, more long-term challenges (such as learning
a new language). You'll probably find that some activities, such
as working to improve your IQ scores, get tougher as you aim higher,
while others, such as amassing new information, might be
difficult to begin with but get easier. Both the thrill of new
challenges and the glow of achievement can boost your
intellectual confidence.

MENTORING

A mentor is someone whom you respect, who has knowledge or wisdom that they can impart to you. Many organizations have mentoring programmes by which people are matched to colleagues who guide their development and progress, but personal intellectual mentoring is too seldom found outside formal education.

Finding a mentor can speed up your expansion of your intellectual capacity. A mentor can help you to see the bigger picture and help you reason through many issues and procedures that might otherwise be difficult to unravel. A good mentor will accelerate your learning, so that you gain a better understanding of the rules or conventions that underpin a discipline (whether it's Shakespearean imagery or economic planning). He or she can help you to explore new areas or see how you can adapt your way of doing things, so that you can work toward achieving goals and broadening your horizons.

Where you turn to for mentoring help is dependent on the subject area and type of support you are looking for. Information sources at the mesosystem and exosystem levels of Bronfenbrenner's "nested systems" (see p.124) are a good starting point.

USING FEEDBACK

The concept of receiving feedback can provide unnecessary difficulty for many people as it often has negative associations with criticism and blame.

THE ART OF LISTENING

Real listening, rather than just nodding and agreeing in the right places, is an art that, when practised, opens up new paths of knowledge, giving your brain food for thought and adding to your stores of information. To listen effectively:

- Give the other person your full attention, and maintain eye contact
- Be non-judgmental
- Allow the person to say everything they need, without being interrupted
- Avoid making assumptions about what they "really" mean
- Briefly paraphrase what you've heard and what you infer, including feelings as well as facts
- Ask questions to make sure you've understood correctly.

However, receiving feedback is vital to learning and therefore to improving your comprehension or depth of understanding of something.

One increasingly popular approach to feedback is the 360 degree assessment, by which employees gain insight into how their work performance is judged by colleagues of different ranks or departments. You could adopt a similar principle by testing your ideas or abilities as broadly as possible.

People who are more experienced or well-informed than yourself can be enlightening, and can alert you to any fallacies in your reasoning. Teaching others is also a form of two-way instruction, as it serves to clarify your own ideas – and a bright listener will always ask thought-provoking questions.

SETTING HEALTHY LIMITS

Underestimating your personal capacity can lead to frustrations and discomfort, but so can over-estimating it. Learning to recognize how far you can reasonably go will actually help you to avoid self-limiting thought processes and enable you to use your skills productively.

KEEPING IT REAL

We're all aware that there are absolute limits to human capacity: few of us are likely to be Olympic athletes or Nobel prize winners. However, we may tantalize ourselves with seemingly more attainable goals, such as becoming a top lawyer *and* a successful novelist. Our fantasies of success in all fields might distract us from applying ourselves sufficiently to any one. Being objective about your limitations can provide you with a realistic framework for your ambitions and prevent you from having to experience a constant stream of disappointment and failure.

MORE AND MORE ABOUT LESS AND LESS

As your mind enquires further and more deeply, it's natural that you might become daunted by the vast expanses of what you don't know or have yet to learn. In fact, the most intellectually gifted people often have the biggest doubts – it's not unusual for leading academics to have an emotional mid-life or mid-career crisis as they find that the more they know, the more they realize they don't know. A narrow approach could lead you to become an expert in a small area of knowledge relatively quickly, and this is satisfying in itself, but as we've seen from the knowledge trees (pp.90–4), every area of knowledge opens up possibilities in other areas that will beg to be explored. Keep a sense of balance: you'll never know everything, but you can still enjoy the wonder and mystery of the world. Aim to become a master of the things you do know and respectful of the things beyond your comprehension.

BEING GOOD ENOUGH

It might seem unlikely, but accepting that you're "good enough" can actually make you perform better. You can remove performance anxiety and more easily enter the "flow" state (see pp. 59–61). This is not a philosophy of compromise, nor is it intended to dismiss excellence, but for most of us in most situations "good" is good enough. Being "good enough" involves trusting your skill and talent – being aware that whatever you have will emerge and perform when you need it to be there for you.

Great actors know that as soon as the curtain rises, their lines will flow: they don't have to worry about it. They can just focus on inhabiting the character. Novice actors, in contrast, worry about the words, pauses, emphasis, where they are on the stage, and the audience. It can be quite disabling to be so wrapped up in the process of performance that it detracts from the flow of talent. Being comfortable with "good enough" enables you to muffle your personal critic and liberate your genius.

CAUSES FOR CELEBRATION

This is my chance to congratulate you for getting this far and for starting your process of personal development. You'll find this journey will enrich both your intellectual capacity and your perception of the world around you.

ONGOING TASKS

We finish this book by considering what ongoing tasks you have to do to enhance your intellectual skills and what you can do to take yourself even further toward creating a more meaningful life.

One major task is to develop your knowledge base. The more extensive your knowledge tree (see pp. 90–4), the easier it will be for you to form mental connections that enable you to assimilate new information. Maintain your expertise by updating your information sources and keeping new information organized (see pp. 123–7).

Your next task is to apply understanding from your areas of expertise to other subjects. This will call on your newly developed ability to think critically, evaluate information and judge how much you need to know to formulate an informed view.

Thirdly, look after your physical well-being. Eat and exercise well, to feed your brain with the nutrients that will help to build the new neural networks that support your enhanced thinking.

BACK TO SCHOOL?
With your new thinking skills under your belt, you may consider one way of making the most of them would be return to further study. Whichever subject you choose, bring all of your enhanced understanding to bear on it. Make your choice with care: you might find some formal courses disappointing. If you're interested in developing your critical capacity, look for a course which involves you in generating new insights and observations. If you want to learn a new skill, find one that allows you to bring your intelligence to bear on practical tasks. If you wish to build your knowledge, look for a course that will add new branches to your knowledge tree (see pp.90–4).

Finally, practise attaining a state of flow (see pp. 59–61). In this state, you'll be more able to use your intellect and your creativity to their fullest extent.

TAKING YOURSELF BEYOND THIS BOOK

As you follow the guidance in this book, you should begin to see the benefits appearing in all areas of your life. Your mastery of new skills and information should increase your confidence, and your successes may embolden you to take risks and aim for new goals and ideals. Your increased ability to see the bigger picture will make the world seem a richer, more fascinating place, and make you better placed to see where you fit into the greater scheme of things. All in all, you should now be able to express the complex, multi-faceted, endlessly adaptable being that you are.

SOLUTIONS

PAGES 25–31: IQ TEST

1 Alike

2 Will

3 Time

4 Travelled

5 ⊔⌐ Notes below the line are negative, above the line are positive. Adding the first and second symbols gives you the third symbol, so −2+4 = +2

6 A. The star moves through a regularly diminishing number of segments – 12, 10, 8 etc – but alternately anticlockwise and clockwise. So the next move would be 4 anticlockwise.

7 15, 14. The sequence is dictated by the 1st, 3rd, 5th etc numbers, which increase by one extra each time: 6+2=8; 8+3=11. The 2nd, 4th, 6th etc numbers are just one less than their predecessor.

8 83. The third number is the sum of the previous two numbers.

9 12. Solving this fast relies on being able to spot a "way in" to the puzzle. In this case it is the 3rd row across: if 4 As are 12, then A must equal 3.

10 24, as it takes a single gardener four hours to mow one lawn. This may be obvious when you take time to think, but working at speed it's easy to assume that if four gardeners take four hours, one gardener takes one hour.

11 D and E

12 Guilty.

13 D2. A has been turned 180° clockwise and tilted backwards to give you view B. Doing the same to C would give you view D2.

14 North once more. (The number of paces is irrelevant.)

PAGES 101–2: INCREASING YOUR POWERS OF LOGIC

1 False. For this conclusion to be correct, you'd have to suppose that every person who favours higher taxes is a socialist – but that supposition is not stated anywhere in the argument.

2 True. Since all whales are mammals, they all have warm blood.

3 This might be true, but only if whiteness were the sole defining feature of swans, and if we knew that no non-white swans existed.

4   This is known as the fallacy of false cause: just because
two events occur together, it doesn't necessarily mean
that they're connected. You'd have to know more
about the hamburger joint, local pest control, and
what Joe is putting in his burgers, in order to
establish any relationship between the two facts.

5   This type of question, called a "complex" question,
is fallacious because it contains an assumption that
hasn't been proved true. (Who says all women are
obsessed with shopping?) Be wary of complex
questions that seem to demand "yes/no" answers
(such as the classic, "Have you stopped beating your
wife yet?").

6   This type of fallacy is known as an appeal to
ignorance: it is the idea that something is true simply
because there's no evidence that it is false, or that
something is false because it hasn't been proved true.
A lack of evidence, by itself, doesn't prove anything.

7   A statement like this is known as an irrelevant
appeal to authority. Such appeals are irrelevant
if they cite the view of someone who is not an
authority in that particular field (Einstein's expertise
was in physics, not ethics), or if there is no need to
cite an expert view (should you really need Einstein
to convince you to be nice?).

8   This type of statement is known as the unfair fallacy.
In rational arguments, it is usually important to try
and see all sides of an issue. However, sometimes
something really is completely right or completely
wrong. For example, could you imagine having an
even-handed discussion on the rights and wrongs
of murder?

FURTHER READING

There are many facets to IQ, and you can read and learn about its history, politics and science alongside understanding IQ from a personal development perspective. The following books are just a few suggestions to pursue in learning about IQ ... and beyond:

Carter, Philip *The Complete Book of Intelligence Tests: 500 exercises to improve, upgrade and enhance your mind strength*, John Wiley & Sons 2005

Gigerenzer, Gerd *Gut Feelings: The intelligence of the unconscious*, Viking/Allen Lane 2007

Hawkins, Jeff and Sandra Blakeslee *On Intelligence*, Owl Books 2005

Herrnstein, Richard J and Charles Murray *The Bell Curve*, Simon & Schuster 1996

Minsky, Marvin *The Emotion Machine: Commonsense thinking, artificial intelligence and the future of the human mind*, Simon & Schuster 2006

Murdoch, Stephen *IQ: A smart history of a failed idea*, John Wiley & Sons 2007

Stafford, Tom and Matt Webb *Mind Hacks: Tips and tricks for using your brain*, O'Reilly 2004

AUTHOR'S WEBSITE

For more information on the author, please visit
www.urbanpsychologist.com

AUTHOR'S ACKNOWLEDGMENTS

Tremendous thanks to all involved in producing this
book, including everyone from DBP, and particularly
to Caroline Ball, who pushed the project to completion
despite my best attempts to procrastinate, avoid and
otherwise delay the proceedings, and to Katie John,
who had the unenviable task of weaving my words and
sentences into a book that is readable and intelligible;
she has a wonderful future.

The lines on pages 107–9 are from Lionel Wade's 1910
translation of Sun Tzu's *The Art of War*.